Cambridge Elements

Elements in Political Psychology
edited by
Yanna Krupnikov
University of Michigan

STRONGER ISSUES, WEAKER PREDISPOSITIONS

Abortion, Gay Rights, and Authoritarianism

Paul Goren
University of Minnesota

CAMBRIDGE
UNIVERSITY PRESS

Shaftesbury Road, Cambridge CB2 8EA, United Kingdom

One Liberty Plaza, 20th Floor, New York, NY 10006, USA

477 Williamstown Road, Port Melbourne, VIC 3207, Australia

314–321, 3rd Floor, Plot 3, Splendor Forum, Jasola District Centre,
New Delhi – 110025, India

103 Penang Road, #05–06/07, Visioncrest Commercial, Singapore 238467

Cambridge University Press is part of Cambridge University Press & Assessment,
a department of the University of Cambridge.

We share the University's mission to contribute to society through the pursuit of
education, learning and research at the highest international levels of excellence.

www.cambridge.org
Information on this title: www.cambridge.org/9781009529310

DOI: 10.1017/9781009529303

© Paul Goren 2024

This publication is in copyright. Subject to statutory exception and to the provisions
of relevant collective licensing agreements, no reproduction of any part may take
place without the written permission of Cambridge University Press & Assessment.

When citing this work, please include a reference to the DOI 10.1017/9781009529303

First published 2024

A catalogue record for this publication is available from the British Library.

ISBN 978-1-009-52931-0 Hardback
ISBN 978-1-009-52932-7 Paperback
ISSN 2633-3554 (online)
ISSN 2633-3546 (print)

Additional resources for this publication at www.cambridge.org/Goren

Cambridge University Press & Assessment has no responsibility for the persistence
or accuracy of URLs for external or third-party internet websites referred to in this
publication and does not guarantee that any content on such websites is, or will
remain, accurate or appropriate.

Stronger Issues, Weaker Predispositions

Abortion, Gay Rights, and Authoritarianism

Elements in Political Psychology

DOI: 10.1017/9781009529303
First published online: December 2024

Paul Goren
University of Minnesota

Author for correspondence: Paul Goren, pgoren@umn.edu

Abstract: Political psychologists have long theorized that authoritarianism structures the positions people take on cultural issues and their party ties. Authoritarianism is durable; it resists the influence of other political judgments; and it is very impactful – in a word, it is strong. By contrast, researchers characterize the attitudes most people hold on most issues as unstable and ineffectual – in a word, weak. But what is true of most issues is not true of the issues that have driven America's long-running culture war – abortion and gay rights. This Element demonstrates that moral issue attitudes are stronger than authoritarianism. With data from multiple sources over the period 1992–2020, it shows that (1) moral issue attitudes endure longer than authoritarianism; (2) moral issues predict change in authoritarianism; (3) authoritarianism does not systematically predict change in moral issues; and (4) moral issues have always played a much greater role than authoritarianism in structuring party ties.

Keywords: political psychology, political science, social psychology, mass communications, sociology

ISBNs: 9781009529310 (HB), 9781009529327 (PB), 9781009529303 (OC)
ISSNs: 2633-3554 (online), 2633-3546 (print)

Contents

An online appendix for this publication at
www.cambridge.org/Goren

1 The Strength of Moral Issues, the Pliability of Authoritarianism

Authoritarianism has purportedly rocked the foundations of American democracy for over two decades. The reservoir of authoritarian sentiment in the mass public has given skilled politicians a chance to win elections by promising to maintain social cohesion and repel threats to the normative order. In 2016, Donald Trump attacked "others" he claimed threatened America's safety and way of life. From his campaign launch speech on June 16, 2015 to his Election Day triumph, Trump smeared Mexican immigrants as dangerous criminals and rapists; pledged to build a wall to bar immigrants at the southern border; called for a ban against Muslims entering the US; toyed with the idea of punishing women who got abortions if the procedure became illegal; made false claims that the murder rate in US cities was the largest in forty-five years; and on and on (Politico 2016). On the campaign trail, he promised to make America great again. In his inaugural address, he vowed to reverse "this American carnage."

Twelve years prior, President George W. Bush drew on the same playbook in his 2004 reelection bid. On February 24, he came out in favor of a constitutional amendment to ban gay marriage, which he framed as a threat to the normative order. Decrying recent moves in San Francisco and Massachusetts to issue marriage licenses for same-sex couples, Bush charged that "[a]fter more than two centuries of American jurisprudence and millennia of human experience, a few judges and local authorities are presuming to change the most fundamental institution of civilization." And with war raging in Iraq, Bush primed the threat of terrorism in the public mind throughout the year. Here is an example from an October 24 campaign speech: "Americans will go to the polls in a time of war and ongoing threats, unlike any we have faced before. The terrorists who killed thousands of innocent people are still dangerous, and they are determined" (Bush 2004, n.p.).

Trump and Bush drew on seemingly distinct issues to mobilize support from the sizable share of the public who held similar views of the world. They were able to do so, the claim goes, because a deep-seated predisposition connects these issues. Political psychologists call this predisposition authoritarianism, which they define as the relative priority people attach to rival sets of core values. Authoritarians favor what Hetherington and Weiler (2018) have called "fixed" values. Authoritarians favor social conformity over personal autonomy; clarity and order over complexity; security over self-direction; and uniformity over diversity. Nonauthoritarians, or libertarians as some call them, hold the reverse set of preferences. They favor "fluid" values over fixed values (Feldman 2003; Stenner 2005; Hetherington and Weiler 2009).[1] That is, they favor personal autonomy, complexity, self-direction, and diversity over conformity, order, security, and uniformity.

In a leading account of authoritarianism and American politics, Hetherington and Weiler (2009) argued that Grand Old Party (GOP) leaders have primed national security, immigration, and cultural issues to secure the support of fixed mindset voters. This strategy advances two key goals – one short-term, the other long-term. The short-term goal is to mobilize enough authoritarian voters to win the next election. The long-term goal is to expand the GOP's electoral coalition. Hetherington and Weiler (2009) have argued that the GOP has succeeded on both counts. From the early 1990s to the present, authoritarian voters have increasingly backed Republican candidates and, starting in 2004, swelled the party's ranks. Journalists and pundits have invoked these findings to explain some of the major developments in American politics these past three decades. These include the changing fortunes of America's political parties; growing racial and ethnic conflict; rising polarization; and Donald Trump's rise to power (Edsall 2018; MacWilliams 2020). As *Vox*'s Amanda Taub wrote in 2016, this research sheds "new light on some of the biggest political stories of the past decade" by showing that authoritarianism "is transforming the Republican Party and the dynamics of national politics" (Taub 2016, n.p.).

The key assumption in this rich vein of work is that authoritarianism operates like a crowning posture in the political minds of everyday Americans. Like other predispositions, it endures over time, resists challenge, and shapes mass political judgment and behavior (Sears 1983; Tesler 2015). More simply, authoritarianism is a strong predisposition. It constrains political attitudes and beliefs that are not as strong. Perhaps the most obvious example here is issue attitudes. Issue attitudes fluctuate erratically over time, move in response to pressure from core predispositions, and wield little influence over party identification (ID) and voter choice. Issue attitudes are weak – so weak that some dismiss them as "nonattitudes" (Converse 1970; Zaller 1992).[2] Because people lack real attitudes on most issues, politicians try to secure voter support by priming the deeper predispositions they believe will give them an electoral edge. This is why GOP candidates embed authoritarian appeals in campaign messages about security and cultural issues.

---

[1] Throughout this Element, I will use fixed values to stand in for authoritarianism and fluid values to denote libertarian values. I will also use "parenting" and "child-rearing" values when talking about the measure.

[2] This claim is not universally accepted. See Fowler (2020) and Simas (2023) for thoughtful dissents.

Of course, a select few issues are stronger than is implied by this account. For example, scholars have noted from time to time that abortion and gay rights seem different. They are "easy" issues that have "moral resonance" which somehow renders them more resilient than other issues (Converse and Markus 1979; Carmines and Stimson 1980; Kinder and Kalmoe 2017). Building on this perspective, Christopher Chapp and I have theorized that attitudes toward abortion and gay rights – which we lump together under the rubric of "moral issues" – are more durable and impactful than nearly all those toward other issues (Goren and Chapp 2017, 2024).[3]

More simply, moral issue attitudes are strong (Krosnick and Petty 1995). Their strength stems from their grounding in automatic, visceral emotions that public discourse has primed since the late 1980s. When those socialized to feel disgust about abortion and gays encounter messages about these issues in public discourse, automatic responses push them in a conservative direction. In contrast, those who have been socialized to feel progressive anger and disgust in the face of attacks on abortion and same-sex individuals respond viscerally with pro-choice, pro-lesbian, gay, bisexual, and transgender (LGBT) sympathies. As these processes recur in a high-intensity-message environment, people's views on moral issues grow stronger. These attitudes become strong enough, Chapp and I argue (Goren and Chapp 2017, 2024), to shape core social and political predispositions when these are misaligned. With data from seven panel studies, we showed that moral issues persist as long as religious and partisan predispositions do; predict change in these predispositions; and sometimes repel their influence (Goren and Chapp 2017, 2024). In short, the instinctual feelings people hold about abortion and same-sex rights are as strong as – or stronger than – the predispositions on which such feelings ostensibly depend. This in turn implies that moral issues play a more central role in structuring the party system and electoral competition than scholars recognize.

If attitudes about abortion and same-sex rights are strong enough to dislodge religious and partisan loyalties, it seems fair to ask if this holds true for other core predispositions. This brings me to the purpose of this Element. My first aim is to sort out, as best I can, the relationship between authoritarianism and moral

---

[3] In this usage of the term, "moral" refers to a specific, narrow class of issues – those grounded in the emotions of moral anger and/or disgust. Other scholars define "moral" issues differently. To take one notable body of work, Ryan (2014, 2017) has theorized that people vary systematically in the moral conviction they attach to various issues. In his usage, "moral" reflects a property of individual attitudes, akin to other properties like attitude certainty or accessibility. Some American voters – by no means all – ground their views toward gay marriage in moral convictions. Others do so for tax cuts or gun control or other issues. Again, Chapp and I (Goren and Chapp 2017, 2024) use "moral" to denote a specific class of issues. There is theoretical value in both approaches – and many others. We make no claim that our usage is preferable.

issue attitudes. I theorize that when cognitive dissonance arises between moral issues and fixed/fluid values, people often resolve the tension by adjusting their values to conform to their feelings about abortion/same-sex rights. My second aim is to show that these issues play a more central role in structuring partisan choice than authoritarianism. Insofar as this is the case, we can conclude that abortion/gay rights drive political conflict in the US to a much greater degree than authoritarianism.

Moving forward, this section covers the following points. Section 1.1 unpacks the logic behind the predisposition-to-attitude models that animate research in political psychology. I then apply this logic to the case of authoritarianism. I elaborate how and why it impacts policy views and party ID. Section 1.2 lays out the theory of moral power, which holds that attitudes toward abortion and gay rights systematically shape core predispositions. Section 1.3 charts the course for the rest of this Element. To preview, I find that moral issues are far more durable and impactful than authoritarianism. By extension, moral issues have played a more central role than authoritarianism in structuring political conflict these past three decades.

1.1 The Conventional View: Authoritarianism Is Strong, Issue Attitudes Are Weak

1.1.1 The Predisposition-to-Issues Model

This section unpacks the standard theoretical take on the relationship between core predispositions and political judgment. Core predispositions hold steady over time; resist challenge; and guide political perception, judgment, and behavior (Zaller 1992). None of this holds true for issue attitudes. This in turn implies that predispositions in general – and core values in particular – shape opinion on most issues. The justification for this causal sequence comes from theories of childhood and adult political development, value-based judgment, and opinion leadership.

I start with developmental theories. The standard claim is that core predispositions emerge in childhood, crystallize during the impressionable years, and harden in adulthood. When children are young, their parents teach them which groups they belong to, what is valuable in life, and what they should believe. As children move into the volatile adolescent years, other forms of influence, such as friends, social media, and real-world events, leave a mark. These socializing agents sometimes modify what is already in place, but they do not eradicate that imprint. Parents still have a lot of success – but not complete success – in passing their core beliefs and values onto their offspring (Jennings and Niemi 1981; Vollebergh et al. 2001; Jennings et al. 2009).

By the time people reach their mid-to-late twenties, their core predispositions have solidified. Once in place, these orientations persist for long spans of time. People accrue a lot of experience seeing the world through these lenses. This does not preclude change, of course. Lifelong openness remains a real possibility for most folks. Some people update their predispositions from time to time in response to major life changes or pressure from other strong dispositions. But such shifts are sporadic and small. Persistence is the rule most of the time (Sears and Brown 2023). Durable predispositions are well-positioned to shape public opinion judgments, party choice, and the vote.

The picture is very different for policy issues. Few people pay more than passing attention to public affairs. Fewer still know what is going on in Washington, DC, their state, and even their local communities. They know even less about specific issues. And whatever they happen to pick up in the news they quickly forget (Price and Zaller 1993; Delli Carpini and Keeter 1996). In the face of such apathy and ignorance, it is no wonder that they fail to develop firm views on issues. Their policy positions bounce around unpredictably over time, shift in response to trivial nudges, and rarely guide voter choice. Since most voting-aged adults lack real views on the issues of the day, they must rely on core predispositions to construct these views on those occasions when their attention turns to politics (Zaller 1992). To put it plainly, issue attitudes are weak.

1.1.2 The Authoritarianism-to-Issues Model

Scholars treat authoritarianism as a core predisposition because it meets the conditions laid out in Section 1.1.1. Fixed/fluid values, like other core values, emerge early in the life cycle, evolve during the impressionable years, stabilize by the mid-twenties, and endure as people age (Kohn et al. 1986; Bubeck and Bilsky 2004; Milfont et al. 2016; Vecchione et al. 2016). Moreover, these values are durable and impactful. Support for authoritarian values predicts Republican identification and GOP votes; hawkish positions on national security issues; anti-immigrant views; pro-life sentiments; and anti-gay stances (Hetherington and Weiler 2009; Cizmar et al. 2014; Smith and Hanley 2018).

These studies rely on cross-sectional data. Analysts must assume that authoritarian/libertarian values structure these choices rather than the other way round. Cross-sectional data preclude testing whether political judgments concurrently shape fixed and fluid values.[4] The fact that values materialize earlier in the life cycle and endure longer than issue attitudes provides some justification for

---

[4] Some recent work has used panel data to try to sort this out, but the verdict is mixed (Bakker et al. 2021; Luttig 2021; Engelhardt et al. 2023). I have more to say about this later on.

assuming that the former shape the latter. But this temporal sequence does not explain why fixed/fluid values shape these choices. Why, specifically, should support for social conformity, social cohesion, and the like engender support for conservative policy positions and attachments to the GOP? Political psychologists have offered two sets of theories in response.

The first set of theories centers on value-based judgment. These theories posit that abstract beliefs about what is good and just in life – that is, values – guide evaluation, judgment, and behavior in many areas of life (Rokeach 1973; Schwartz 1994; Miles 2015). These include personal judgments, such as group attachments, religious behavior, career choice, intergroup contact, and many other things (Sagiv et al. 2017). In the same way, the political judgments people make reflect trade-offs between fixed and fluid values, as well as other trade-offs that involve different values. The views we express on social and political issues reflect the values we hold dear; signal to others what we think is important in life; and let us affirm how we see ourselves (Feldman 1988; Goren et al. 2016).

Let's take a look at how this works for authoritarian values and moral issues. At the most basic level, disputes over abortion and same-sex rights boil down to what is best for individuals versus what is best for society – that is, disputes about desirable modes of conduct and end-states of existence (Rokeach 1973). Among those who place a lot of value on conformity and uniformity, opposition to abortion and gays/gay rights expresses these commitments. In their minds, abortion and same-sex relations violate clear-cut standards of right and wrong; they undermine unity; and they disrupt the social order. For those who instead prioritize personal autonomy and diversity, having limits on abortion and gay rights is a nonstarter. These folks see such limits as illegitimate restrictions on personal freedom and unjust efforts to stamp out differences. In these examples, there is a natural fit between fixed/fluid values and positions on moral issues. As Feldman (2020, 42) has put it, "there may be a relatively constant association between authoritarianism and conservative positions on social/moral issues like abortion [and] gay marriage."

A second set of theories explains how and why fixed/fluid values undergird the stances people take on culture war issues. Theories of opinion leadership rest on a simple and powerful logic. When political elites frame issues in terms of deeper values, many citizens learn "what goes with what" (Converse 1964; Zaller 1992). The frames that elites deploy teach people how to connect discrete issues to particular values. Leaders do this because they think the frames they choose will help them in the court of public opinion, to triumph in the next election and/or to grow their constituency over time.

Hetherington and Weiler (2009) have drawn on this approach to explain the evolution of electoral politics and the party system from the 1960s to the present day. Republican elites have taken conservative positions on national security, race, immigration, and social issues for a long time. The effect of GOP messaging on these issues, along with Democratic pushback, has been twofold. First, by priming these issues and framing them in the language of fixed/fluid values, political elites have taught voters to see these issues through the lens of authoritarianism. In this way, top-down elite messaging has reinforced the bottom-up affinity between fixed values and right-wing issue positions. The GOP messaging has helped big swaths of the electorate learn that if they hold authoritarian values, they should oppose abortion and gay rights. Simultaneously, fluid value voters have learned that they should back abortion and same-sex rights.

Second, by taking conservative positions on these and other issues, GOP leaders have signaled that it is the natural home for authoritarians. Here, the GOP messaging has heightened the party's appeal to those who prefer social conformity to personal autonomy, uniformity to diversity, and so on. This helped the GOP break the Democratic Party's iron-clad grip over the federal government from the early 1930s through the mid-1960s. The net result has been "a coalitional reconfiguration of the parties ... with authoritarians increasingly gravitating toward the Republican Party and nonauthoritarians increasingly gravitating toward the Democratic Party" (Hetherington and Weiler 2009, 158). More simply, authoritarians sorted into the GOP. Libertarians moved into the Democratic camp. In this account, it is values, whether fixed or fluid, that drive people into parties.

To sum up, this influential line of work holds that authoritarianism functions like a bedrock predisposition in the political minds of most citizens. Fixed/fluid values sit at the head of a causal chain where they constrain a wide range of political judgments and choices – party ID and policy attitudes most notably. Authoritarianism is a "normative 'worldview' about the social value of obedience and conformity (or freedom and difference), the prudent and just balance between group authority and individual autonomy" (Stenner 2005, 17). As a worldview, authoritarianism "is situated near the beginning of the causal chain of political reasoning where it will serve as a determinant of public opinion and political behavior" (Hetherington and Weiler 2009, 36). As a prime mover of public opinion and political behavior, authoritarianism has driven political conflict in the country for the past generation and shows little sign of abating in the future. Indeed, its hold on American politics has grown by leaps and bounds during the Trump era.[5]

---

[5] Christopher M. Federico, Stanley Feldman, and Christopher Weber are currently working on a book manuscript on this subject: "Change and Resistance: How Authoritarianism Structures Political Conflict in the United States."

1.2 An Alternative View

1.2.1 The Theory of Moral Power

In this section, I argue that attitudes toward the two key issues that have epitomized America's ongoing culture war – abortion and gay rights – do not fit the standard theory. I begin with a formal definition. By moral issue attitudes, I mean summary judgments about abortion and gay rights. These judgments are bottom-line evaluations of both issues (Eagly and Chaiken 2007). Some people hold positive views of abortion and equal rights for same-sex individuals. I call them moral progressives. Others reject abortion and gay rights. Let's call them moral conservatives.

This conceptualization melds all facets of these two issues into a single construct. The rationale for doing so is simple. If you support abortion rights in one situation (i.e., the woman's life is in danger), you're likely to favor reproductive rights in another situation (i.e., the woman is single and does not want to get married). And if you back abortion rights like these, you're more likely to back same-sex marriage and antidiscrimination laws than a staunch pro-lifer is. That said, some readers may still object to this conceptual admixture. In Section 2, I make a strong empirical case for joining them together this way.

As I remarked earlier, a handful of studies have hinted that views on moral issues are stronger than views on other issues (Converse and Markus 1979; Carmines and Stimson 1980; Kinder and Kalmoe 2017). For the most part, political psychologists have not explored what makes these issues different and why it matters for politics. In reply, Christopher Chapp and I have proposed a theory that we believe answers these questions in ways that are clear and convincing (Goren and Chapp 2017, 2024). Our theory of moral power contends that moral issue attitudes are as strong as the core predispositions on which they ostensibly depend.

The theory rests on four propositions. (1) Since the late 1980s, the information environment has furnished voting-aged adults with lots of chances to evaluate abortion and gay rights. (2) As messages about these issues have flowed through the information environment, those who received the messages experienced automatic emotional reactions that nudged them to respond in a consistent way. For some, conservative moral disgust pushed them to evaluate abortion and gay rights negatively. For others, messages that attacked women and gays elicited progressive anger and disgust that fed pro-choice, pro-gay sympathies. This mix of high message intensity and visceral emotional responding stabilized moral issue attitudes and infused them with the power to drive change in core predispositions. (3) For all their stability, predispositions are not permanent. They move in response to pressure from other strong attitudes and beliefs. (4) When conflicts between core predispositions and moral issues come to the fore, some people resolve the dissonance by adjusting their predispositions to fit their issue tastes.[6]

Chapp and I have uncovered some evidence consistent with these claims (Goren and Chapp 2017, 2024). First, moral issue messaging in political and nonpolitical discourses ratcheted up starting in the late 1980s and has remained high ever since. Second, moral issue attitudes have proved to be as stable as, and sometimes more stable than, religious ID and party ID. None of these idea elements were fixed. Third, our panel data analyses found that moral issues predict party and religious change four to six years later. Of note, the effects of moral issues on party ID were over twice as large as the effects of party ID on issues. This finding supports the conclusion that moral issues are stronger than party ID. More broadly, the cumulative pattern of results demonstrates that Americans' feelings about abortion and gay rights are durable, hard to move, and impactful – they are strong (Krosnick and Petty 1995).

1.2.2 The Moral Issue Attitudes-to-Authoritarianism Model

This Element takes up the question of whether attitudes on abortion/same-sex rights affect authoritarianism in similar ways. To the degree that authoritarianism operates like a worldview, this is a hard test for the theory of moral power. Attitudes depend on worldviews; they do not structure worldviews. This in turn implies that worldviews undergird political evolution and issue agendas in the party system. But if moral issues shape this worldview, the way we characterize the party system necessarily changes to one in which abortion and gay rights take on elevated importance.

Can moral issue attitudes really shape authoritarianism? There are two reasons to expect that they can. First, although values like conformity, security, and self-direction hold steady, they do not endure indefinitely. A brief review of some published work makes this point plain. First, Schuster et al.'s (2019) overview of research on value stability speaks directly to this point. They reported that rank-order correlations for basic human values – including some

---

[6] The theory of moral power ignores the possibility that individual differences might shape the crystallization of moral attitudes. To take one example, Margolis (2018) stresses the importance of attitude crystallization during formative periods in early adulthood. It would be useful here to probe variation in attitude structures and effects across generational cohorts. The theoretical setup would suggest that Americans who came of age (politically speaking) in the late 1980s and beyond might evince stronger attitudes toward moral issues than respondents who grew up in earlier decades. Attitudes toward abortion/gays may be less stable and less consequential for individuals whose formative years did not feature as much extreme emotional mobilization around these issues. Given space limitations, I do not address this. This is an area ripe for future exploration.

fixed and fluid values – fell in the range of 0.51 to 0.82 for periods of one to eight years.[7] The upper estimates are similar to what we find in the case of moral issues, party ID, and religious orientations (Goren and Chapp 2017, 2024).

Some of the values that are covered in Schuster et al.'s (2019) review are similar to authoritarian values studied by political psychologists. But since the values in Schuster et al. (2019) are not identical, it is natural to wonder if the standard measure of authoritarianism also proves stable over time.[8] Here, I am referring to the four child-rearing items that have appeared on American National Election Studies (ANES) surveys since 1992. I have a lot more to say about this measure in Section 2. For now, I simply point to the work of Englehardt et al. (2023). Using data from two panel studies that spanned eight and fourteen months, they reported an average continuity correlation of 0.70. When they purged random error from these scales, the mean correlation leapt to 0.92. These are strong correlations. At the same time, they still leave some room for change.

Given that fixed/fluid values evolve to some degree over time, the key question is whether moral issue attitudes facilitate some of that evolution. On its face, the claim that issue attitudes drive change in core predispositions is not credible for most issues because most issue attitudes are weak. But abortion and gay rights are not most issues. They are much stronger – more durable and more impactful – than other issues. This suggests a pathway through which moral issue attitudes can induce change in fixed/fluid values. This path centers on the resolution of cognitive dissonance (Festinger 1957; Campbell et al. 2021). When attitudes and beliefs conflict with one another, the ensuing tension leads to some mental discomfort. To relieve it, people must locate the source. When they locate it, the fix is simple. Bring the attitudes and beliefs into alignment by revising one of them to conform to the other.

Value theorists have made these points. They argue that values endure over time, but also change under some conditions (Rokeach 1973; Schwartz 1992). Major life changes, such as the birth of a child or the death of a spouse, can spark value change. Values also evolve slowly in response to the mundane pressures of work or broader social and cultural changes (Kohn 1977; Putnam and Campbell 2010). Building on these perspectives, Bardi and Goodwin (2011) have developed a model of value change that ties change back to the information environment. If people receive a series of messages that implicate a set of values, value change may result when they conflict with related attitudes and beliefs. Some message recipients resolve the dissonance by updating their

---

[7] Some of these estimates, but not all, corrected for measurement error in the survey responses.

[8] Schuster et al. (2019) looked at the Schwartz measures of conformity, security, and self-direction values.

attitudes and beliefs. But others react the other way. They adjust their values to conform to strong attitudes or beliefs. Goren (2004) and Connors (2020) provide evidence that political values bend in response to some social and psychological pressures. In short, we cannot presume that people always resolve cognitive dissonance in favor of values.

In the case of moral issues, the information environment has delivered numerous signals over the past three decades. These signals began to multiply at the end of the 1980s. Message volume has remained high since then. This holds true in prominent political mediums. But, to an unusual degree, messages about abortion and same-sex rights have spilled over into many nonpolitical outlets. To document these trends, Goren and Chapp (2024) analyzed (1) party platforms from 1972 to 2020; (2) more than 119,000 newspaper articles; (3) over 56,000 congressional speeches; (4) some 6,100 congressional campaign websites; (5) 6,600 television (TV) episodes; (6) 1,500-plus Christian sermons; and (7) select highway billboards in three states. While this does not provide a complete account of moral issue messaging in the current era, it does suggest that public discourse – defined broadly – has primed moral issue attitudes in the public mind for decades.

At the same time, this ongoing discourse has presumably primed fixed/fluid values, which helps to explain how these values came to structure moral issues in Hetherington and Weiler's (2009) account. While GOP candidates and leaders have taken conservative positions on culture war issues for a long time, the Democrats have responded in kind. These messages, along with the attendant media coverage, have reinforced the natural connections between fixed/fluid values and moral issues at the individual level. Since these messages have activated both moral issues and authoritarianism in the public mind, many people have no doubt felt some cognitive dissonance due to value–attitude conflict. This in turn raises the possibility that some folks have resolved this tension by amending their core values to reflect how they feel about abortion rights and gay rights.

In sum, my chief theoretical claim is that as the information ecosystem routinely primed these issues, it brought to light conflicts between moral issues and authoritarianism. Some conflicted souls reduced this dissonance by updating their values to reflect their deep-seated feelings about abortion and same-sex rights. In this way, strong feelings about moral issues structure authoritarianism.

What might value change look like in practice? Here is an example of what I have in mind. Imagine someone who long valued social conformity over personal autonomy. At the same time, she supported gay marriage, gay rights, and abortion under most circumstances. Her policy views have not wavered with the passage of time. Over the years, the GOP's pro-life stance and coolness toward gay rights, along with Democratic Party pushback and the attendant media coverage, have ensured that both issues remain accessible in her mind. When these messages activated her issue attitudes, these attitudes diverged from her preference for conformity over autonomy. The tension grew increasingly uncomfortable. Ultimately, she resolved the tension by updating her value preferences. She came to attach a bit more importance to autonomy and diversity. This is an example of issue-driven value change. One can readily imagine similar sorts of changes.

1.3 What Structures Political Conflict

Does any of this matter more broadly? How does sorting this out advance our understanding of American politics? These theories take fundamentally different views about the central elements in mass belief systems. In so doing, they diverge on what drives conflict in the political system. If we gain leverage over how these idea elements fit together in the minds of individuals, we learn something about elections, campaigns, and the party system.

To illustrate the distinct structures implied by the two theories, Figure 1 employs a pair of path diagrams. There are four variables in the model: authoritarianism, party ID, moral issue attitudes, and candidate evaluations. Path model (a) in Figure 1 reflects the prevailing view in much of political psychology and political science. In this take, authoritarianism is the central orientation – the "crowning posture," to use Converse's (1964) felicitous phrase. Fixed/fluid values structure party ID, the positions people take on moral issues, and their candidate evaluations. Values further manifest indirect effects throughout the model. First, they shape moral issues via their influence on party ID. Second, they shape candidate evaluations through party ID. Third, values affect candidate evaluation via the party-to-issues-to-candidate evaluation path. Last, they also indirectly impact candidate preferences via their effects on moral issues. Insofar as this model is consistent with the evidence, analysts can conclude that authoritarianism functions like a worldview.

Model (b) in Figure 1 displays the theory of moral power. Here, moral issues crown the belief system hierarchy. Attitudes toward abortion/gay rights directly shape authoritarianism, party loyalties, and candidate preferences. These feelings also indirectly shape candidate preferences via fixed/fluid values and party ID. The gray path that runs from authoritarianism to party ID reflects uncertainty about whether the former causes the latter. The theory of moral power entertains this possibility. It does not assume it.

(a) Authoritarianism as the crowning posture

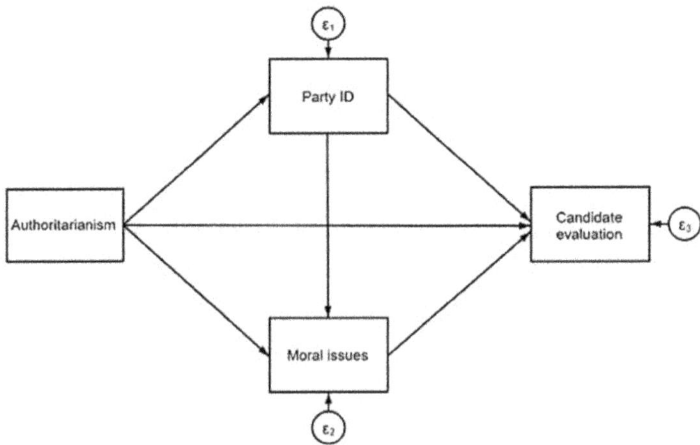

(b) Moral issue attitudes as the crowning posture

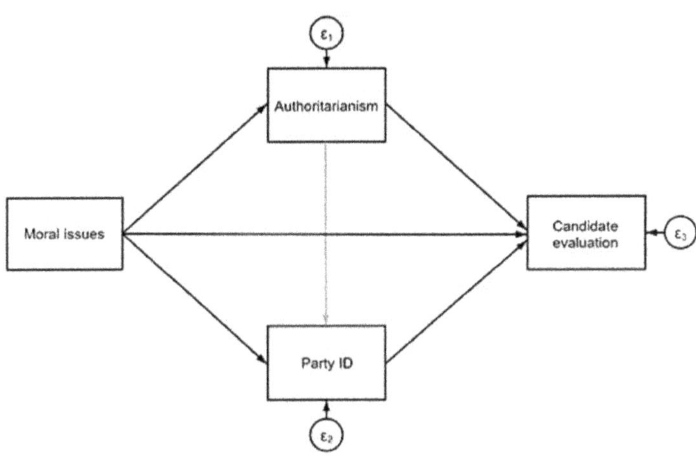

Figure 1 Alternative models of belief system structure.

If the evidence favors model (b) over model (a) (see Figure 1), then the claim that moral issues drive broader political conflict becomes credible.[9]

---

[9] I offer some qualifications at this point. First, Figure 1 is, to put it mildly, greatly oversimplified. It provides a bare bones sketch of belief system structure. It ignores other issues that people feel strongly about, such as immigration. It ignores other predispositions, such as racial prejudice and social identities. There are no feedback loops, no moderators. In response, I stress that my aim is

Such evidence would suggest that differences between moral conservatives and progressives structure the party system and elections more than differences between authoritarians and nonauthoritarians do. It would also suggest that candidates talk about issues like these because voters care about them, not because the issues activate latent beliefs about conformity, diversity, and order. To finish up, learning how fixed/fluid values and moral issues affect one another in the minds of voters has the potential to shed new light on broader political dynamics.

Note that space limitations preclude analysis of all pathways in models (a) and (b) of Figure 1. As such, I restrict my analysis to the links between moral issues, authoritarianism, and party ID – the antecedents of candidate choice. Sorting this out is a necessary first step before moving on to the explanation of candidate evaluations.

1.4 Organization of the Element

Here is my roadmap for working all of this out. Section 2 takes up the measurement of authoritarianism and moral issue positions. The most widely used set of authoritarianism items – the child-rearing battery – has appeared on ANES surveys since 1992. The General Social Survey (GSS) has some serviceable items as well. I argue that they are all valid and reliable measures of the same latent construct. Then, with new data from a 2020 YouGov survey I show that responses to the ANES and GSS items fit a one-factor model, indicating that the responses derive from the same latent predisposition. This supports the use of ANES and GSS data in the rest of the Element. Section 2 then pivots to the abortion and gay rights items that populate these surveys. I show that responses to these items derive from two closely related factors that, in turn, reflect the same attitudinal disposition. This provides the justification I need to combine abortion and gay rights items into summary scales.

In Section 3, I describe the panel data sets and then deploy these to assess the stability of fixed/fluid values and moral issues. I gauge stability using continuity correlations and tabular data. Across the board, moral issue opinions prove much more stable than parenting values. Section 4 uses the panel data to estimate models of value and issue change. I show that lagged authoritarianism does not predict change in moral issue positions until the Trump years.

---

to take a first step in advancing the case that attitudes toward abortion/gay rights are stronger – and authoritarianism is perhaps weaker – than currently believed. The second qualification follows from the first. While I often use causal language in the Element, I recognize that the statistical evidence I bring to bear on the issues–values relationship does not permit definitive causal inferences. By using multiple panel data sets from different time periods and different statistical estimators, I can make stronger claims about how the key variables are related than prior work can. This adds value, but, again, causal proof is not possible with the observational data at my disposal.

In contrast, lagged issue opinions predict change in authoritarianism from the early 1990s to the present time. Section 5 builds the case for the strength of moral issues by looking at the effects each variable has on party ID. I do so in both cross-sectional and panel data. The results are unequivocal. Moral issues move party ID to a far greater extent than authoritarianism. This result holds in every data set I examine. In sum, Sections 3–5 show that moral issues are (1) more durable than authoritarianism; (2) harder to change than authoritarianism; and (3) more impactful than authoritarianism.

Section 6 brings this Element to a close. There, I briefly recap the key findings. The rest of the section takes up the implications my findings have for understanding public opinion and belief system structure at the micro-level and political competition and conflict at the macro-level.

2 The Measurement of Authoritarianism and Moral Issues

This section describes the measures I use to test the hypotheses in later sections. The typical practice is to relegate measurement to a short section embedded in a larger section that covers other materials. I refrain from doing so here for two reasons. First, in subsequent sections I use ANES and GSS data to test the key hypotheses. Political psychologists view the ANES measures as the disciplinary benchmark. Scholars do not rely heavily on the GSS measures, so there is presumably less knowledge about – and less confidence in – these items (see Stenner 2005 for a notable exception). As such, I need to build the case that the GSS items are valid and reliable measures of latent fixed/fluid values. To do so, I use new data from a 2020 YouGov survey to show that responses to the ANES and GSS items are moderately to highly correlated and derive from the same latent impulse. These estimates provide the justification needed to use the GSS data and trust the results.

The other reason I devote a section to measurement centers on my claim that opinions about abortion and same-sex rights derive from the same attitudinal source. While there is some support for this in extant work (see Jelen 2009), I suspect that readers would prefer to see direct evidence in lieu of a citation to a review essay. I provide this evidence here. I show that responses to these items derive from two closely related factors that, in turn, reflect a broader attitudinal disposition. This allows me to merge answers to questions on abortion and gay rights into simple additive scales.

2.1 Measuring Authoritarianism

Scholars have been studying authoritarianism since the 1950s. Adorno et al. (1950) developed the first set of questions. Although their F-scale (F for fascist) correlated with a number of outcome variables as expected, critics have identified a number of problems with that scale. Altemeyer's (1981) Right Wing Authoritarianism (RWA) scale became the new standard and served as a workhorse variable for a number of years. Though much improved over the original F-scale, critics have found faults with the RWA scale too (for the details, see Feldman 2003 and Stenner 2005).

In response, Feldman and Stenner (1997) introduced a new set of items. These items tap into beliefs about child-rearing values and have appeared on many ANES surveys from 1992 onward. The items begin with this prompt: "Although there are a number of qualities that people feel that children should have, every person thinks that some are more important than others. I am going to read you pairs of desirable qualities. For each pair please tell me which one you think is more important for a child to have." The pairs are:

- independence or respect for elders
- obedience or self-reliance
- curiosity or good manners
- being considerate or being well-behaved.

When survey respondents choose "elders," "obedience," "good manners," and "well-behaved," they signal support for conformity, obedience, clarity, and uniformity. These are the fixed or authoritarian values described in Section 1. On the flip side, "independence," "self-reliance," "curiosity," and "considerate" get at fluid values. These responses reflect support for self-direction, autonomy, and diversity – the libertarian values.

These items have several desirable properties. First, they directly tap into the trade-offs that define the fixed–fluid worldview divide. These include the trade-offs between social conformity and personal autonomy; obedience and freedom; uniformity and diversity; and order/clarity versus accepting shades of gray. Second, because these items do not reference specific groups, issues, or current political debates, responses to them are not contaminated by political content. Third, the validation work done on behalf of these scales is convincing. These scales correlate with measures of related concepts in ways we would expect; the responses people give to these questions hold steady over time; and the items combine to produce fairly reliable scales (Feldman 2003; Hetherington and Weiler 2009; Englehardt et al. 2023). One limitation is that the forced-choice item format makes it hard to distinguish between those who hold strong versus not very strong views in the ends of the scale.

Another set of child-rearing items has appeared on GSS surveys dating back to the 1970s. The most recent iteration of this battery begins with this prompt: "If you had to choose, which thing on this list would you pick as the most important for a child to learn to prepare him or her for life?" Respondents then rank-order five values: "to obey," "to be well-liked or popular," "to think for himself or herself," "to work hard," and "to help others when they need help." Those who rank "to obey" higher than "to think for himself or herself" count as authoritarian. Those who do the reverse are libertarian.

Like the ANES items, the GSS measures get at the tensions between social conformity and personal autonomy, between obedience and self-direction, in a very straightforward manner. Also, the GSS items make no reference to specific groups, issues, or policy controversies. These are hallmarks of an effective and unobtrusive measurement strategy. Stenner (2005) has done a thorough job validating these scales. With eight scale points, this two-item scale makes fine-grained distinctions between those who strongly prefer conformity over autonomy or vice versa. Its major shortcoming lies in not directly tapping into other value trade-offs (e.g., uniformity versus diversity).

The ANES and GSS measures seem quite similar on their face. Insofar as both sets of items tap into fixed/fluid values, I can rely on data from both sources to test the empirical implications of the standard and alternative theories. But it is not clear if both sets of items do in fact tap into latent authoritarianism to a similar degree. To sustain the claim that they do, two sorts of evidence would help. First, the answers people give to these items should correlate moderately to highly. Second, these correlations should be high enough to come from a single latent factor.

To test these predictions, I collected data from a 2020 YouGov survey.[10] The data come from the October wave (wave 2) of a three-wave, multi-investigator panel survey carried out that election season. My module included the standard ANES and GSS parenting items described just now. Following common practice, I dropped African Americans from the sample (Pérez and Hetherington 2014).[11] To begin, Table 1 reports the correlations.[12] The first four items use the standard ANES wording. The fifth and sixth items use the GSS wording.[13] Positive correlations mean that subjects who give an authoritarian response to one question usually do the same to the other question. I expect the pairwise correlations between the ANES and the GSS items to be big enough to suggest mutual dependence on the same construct.

---

[10] The University of Minnesota's College of Liberal Arts and its Center for the Study of Political Psychology funded the survey.

[11] Pérez and Hetherington (2014, 410) report that "using parenting preferences to measure authoritarianism across racial groups is problematic" because Blacks and Whites understand the survey items differently. In light of this, I dropped African Americans from all the statistical analyses in the Element. But note that when I include African Americans in the samples, the general pattern of results does not change significantly.

[12] I report tetrachoric/polychoric correlations, which are appropriate for categorical and dichotomous variables like these.

[13] The "think for self" item is reverse coded.

Table 1 A correlation matrix for the ANES and GSS child-rearing items, 2020 YouGov non-Black respondents

	Independence/elders	Obey/self	Curiosity/ manners	Considerate/ well-behaved	Obey	Think for self
ANES Independence/elders	1.00					
ANES Obey/self-reliance	0.62	1.00				
ANES Curiosity/manners	0.68	0.63	1.00			
ANES Considerate/well-behaved	0.46	0.56	0.54	1.00		
GSS Obey	0.49	0.55	0.50	0.40	1.00	
GSS Think for self (reverse coded)	0.41	0.43	0.39	0.34	0.55	1.00

Notes: All correlations are significant at $p < 0.01$. The table reports tetrachoric and polychoric correlations. Mean correlation = 0.50. The polychoric correlation between an additive ANES scale (items 1–4) and an additive GSS scale (items 5–6) = 0.56. Number of cases = 1,334.

Source: 2020 YouGov survey.

The initial returns are encouraging. Moderate-to-strong correlations emerge across the board. These range from a low of 0.34 to a high of 0.68. The mean correlation comes out to 0.50. When I focus on the association between the ANES and the GSS items, these range from 0.34 to 0.55 and average a solid 0.44. To be sure, this average trails the mean ANES item correlation ($r = 0.58$) and the GSS correlation ($r = 0.55$). That said, the data reveal that the answers people give to the ANES and GSS questions are fairly consistent. People who place a lot of value on teaching children "to obey" also favor "respect for elders" over "independence," "good manners" over "curiosity," and so on. Likewise, those who want a child "to think for himself or herself" often prefer "self-reliance" to "obedience" and "considerate" to "well-behaved."[14] While these results are encouraging, this evidence cannot tell us if the answers people give to the ANES and GSS items derive from the same underlying impulse.

My expectation is that the responses arise from the same source. To test this, I turn to confirmatory factor analysis (CFA) techniques. This method provides evidence on whether a single underlying factor or multiple factors generate the patterns we see in correlation matrices like that in Table 1. I started with a one-factor model.[15] The model included correlated errors between the two GSS items. The error correlation captures variance that these items share with each other but not with the ANES items. Shared variance likely arises from the question format.

Table 2 has the results. The aim here is to specify a model that reproduces the observed correlation matrix as accurately as possible. A statistically insignificant chi-square test result indicates success. Here, the chi-square test comes in at $p = 0.12$. The estimates from three goodness-of-fit statistics indicate that a one-factor model fits the data very well: NNFI = 0.97, SRMR = 0.02, RMSEA = 0.08 (Hu and Bentler 1999).[16] Turning to the factor loadings, we can see that the unstandardized estimates are uniformly high and similar in magnitude with the exception of the GSS "think for oneself" item, which comes in a bit lower. The factor loadings range from 0.66 to 1.06. The standardized loadings vary from 0.52 to 0.84. The latter reflect moderate-to-strong correlations between the responses people give to these items and the underlying factor.

Overall, the YouGov data show that all pairwise correlations lie in the moderate-to-strong range and that a single factor accounts for them.

---

[14] Note also that the correlation between a four-item ANES scale and a two-item GSS scale is 0.56.

[15] I applied the unweighted least squares (ULS) estimator to the polychoric correlation matrix in Table 1. Simulation work shows that this estimator works as well as other categorical estimators (Forero et al. 2009; Rhemtulla et al. 2012).

[16] The three goodness-of-fit measures are: NNFI = non-normed fit index; SRMR = standardized root mean squared residual; and RMSEA = root mean square error of approximation.

Table 2 A CFA model for the ANES and GSS child-rearing values, 2020 YouGov non-Black respondents

	Estimates
ξ_1 Authoritarianism	
λ_1 ANES Independence/respect elders	1.00
	0.78
λ_2 ANES Obedience/self-reliance	1.06
	0.82
λ_3 ANES Curiosity/good manners	1.04
	0.81
λ_4 ANES Considerate/well-behaved	0.84
	0.65
λ_5 GSS Obey ranking	0.82
	0.64
λ_6 GSS Think for oneself ranking (reverse coded)	0.66
	0.52
Model fit:	
Satorra-Bentler corrected χ^2 / 8 degrees of freedom	12.64
χ^2 p value	0.12
NNFI	0.97
SRMR	0.02
RMSEA	0.08
Number of observations	1,334

Notes: Robust categorical ULS estimates based on polychoric correlations. Unstandardized factor loadings reported, with standardized loadings in italics. All parameter estimates are significant at $p < 0.01$. The model includes a correlated error term between Items 5 and 6 to capture method-induced covariance.

Source: 2020 YouGov survey.

This evidence supports the claim that the two GSS parenting items can serve as valid, if imperfect, measures of authoritarianism. Again, compared to the four-item ANES scale, the two-item GSS scale provides less coverage of the domain of content – a relative disadvantage. But the GSS scale has one critical advantage over its ANES counterpart. With eight points compared to five for the ANES scale, the GSS scale can better distinguish between strong and not very strong authoritarians (and libertarians). In closing, I conclude that the ANES and the GSS items tap the same latent impulse – authoritarianism. The evidence reported here provides the justification I need in order to use the GSS measures of child-rearing values. This in turn opens up many more opportunities to test hypotheses about the impact and endogeneity of authoritarianism.

2.2 Measuring Attitudes Toward Moral Issues

I have defined moral issue attitudes as bottom-line evaluations of abortion *and* gay rights. Since these are distinct issues, some may be uneasy with this conceptual blend. They will want to see evidence that opinions about both issues form a coherent whole. Here, I provide such evidence.

I use multiple items to tap into moral issues in each data set. This approach has two advantages over single items. First, multiple items provide wider-ranging coverage of the domain of content than single measures, thereby improving measurement validity. For example, a respondent might approve of abortion in the case of rape but not if the woman doesn't want any more children. If we rely on her answer to the first question and ignore her second response, we misclassify her as pro-choice. If we employ only her second response, we misclassify her as pro-life. But with both answers we procure a more accurate (albeit imperfect) read of her mixed feelings about abortion. The same logic applies to gay rights. Someone might favor gays in the military but oppose marriage for same-sex couples. If we rely on their first response, we classify this person as pro–gay rights. If we use only their second response, they count as anti-gay. Under each scenario, we mismeasure the underlying attitude. By employing the answers to both questions, we can accurately gauge the respondent's ambivalence about same-sex rights.

The use of multiple measures has a second advantage. Multi-item scales are more reliable than single items (Ansolabehere et al. 2008). Reliability means the degree to which a set of opinion items yields consistent results on repeated application to different cases (or to the same cases over time). When opinion scales prove reliable, they do a good job capturing the underlying attitude by minimizing the intrusion of random measurement error (RME) in the responses. Reliable measures, in short, capture far more signal than noise.

Here, I review the abortion and gay rights items used throughout this Element. First, the number of items in a given scale ranges from two to twelve. Second, every survey contains a mix of abortion and gay rights items. Most of the ANES surveys contain a single abortion item, except the 2012–2013 ANES, which has eight. The ANES surveys also contain a handful of questions about gay marriage and gay rights. Each GSS survey contains seven yes/no questions about abortion and two questions about gays and lesbians. For gay rights, the

GSS asks about same-sex relations and homosexual marriage. These are categorical items. Third, the issue content of the scales is often imbalanced. Some scales contain more abortion items. Others have more gay rights items. Fourth, as documented in Section 2.3, scale reliability varies from acceptable to exceptional. Readers who want to review question wording should check out the online appendix.

If opinions about abortion and gay rights spring from the same attitudinal basis, then the items should, at a minimum, correlate moderately to strongly. People who favor abortion in one scenario should usually favor it in a second distinct case. As well, pro-choice folks should be more apt to back equal rights for gays and lesbians than pro-life folks. To test these claims, I turn to data from the 2006 GSS and the 2012 ANES cross-sectional surveys. Note that the same pattern of results is present in other data sets.

Per Cook et al. (1992), I distinguish between "traumatic" and "elective" abortion circumstances. In the GSS data, the traumatic items refer to health risks, birth defects, and rape. For example: "The woman's own health is seriously endangered by the pregnancy." Elective items revolve around lifestyle preferences. For instance: "She is not married and does not want to marry the man." I created a simple additive scale of traumatic abortions using the "woman's health," "rape," and "serious defect" items and a second scale for elective abortions based on the "any reason," "does not want more children," "low income," and "doesn't want to marry the man" items.

Table 3 reports the pairwise polychoric correlations in the 2006 GSS data set – again, focusing on non-Black respondents. If the answers people give to these questions spring from the same latent attitude, we should find robust positive correlations. This is indeed what I find. The two strongest pairwise correlations emerge for the abortion mini-scales ($r = 0.84$) and the gay rights variables ($r = 0.78$). So far, so good. Just as importantly, the correlations between the abortion and the gay rights items prove solid, ranging from 0.46 to 0.55. The mean correlation across the six pairs equals 0.61. The table reveals that many people consistently took pro-choice, pro-gay stances. Others routinely opposed these rights. The patterns hint that the opinions people give in response to abortion and gay rights questions derive from a single latent attitude.

To test this hypothesis, I apply CFA techniques to the correlation matrix. If a single latent attitude guides the responses people give, a one-factor solution will emerge. If the abortion items and gay rights items derive from separate attitudinal dimensions, we'll see a two-factor solution. While the latter result would not be consistent with my claim that responses derive from the same latent factor, there could be justification for combining the items into a single

Table 3 A polychoric correlation matrix for abortion and gay rights items, 2006 GSS non-Black respondents

	Traumatic abortions	Elective abortions	Homosexual relations	Gay marriage
Traumatic abortions	1.00			
Elective abortions	0.84	1.00		
Homosexual relations	0.55	0.54	1.00	
Gay marriage	0.46	0.47	0.78	1.00

Notes: All correlations significant at $p < 0.01$. Mean correlation = 0.61. Number of cases = 1,471. Very similar results were obtained in the 2008, 2010, 2012, and 2014 GSS cross-sections. Probability weights used.

scale if the correlation between the latent factors is sufficiently high to suggest dependence on a higher-order factor.[17]

Initial efforts to fit a one-factor solution revealed poor model fit. I then specified a two-factor model, constraining the traumatic and the elective abortion scales to load on one factor and the two gay rights items to load on a separate, correlated factor. Table 4 reports these estimates. The two-factor model fits the data very well. The global chi-square is insignificant, which supports the inference that the two-factor model holds in the population. The NNFI and SRMR values are excellent, while the RMSEA is subpar.[18] Next, the loadings are statistically significant, substantively powerful, and similar in magnitude. The standardized loadings vary from 0.81 to 0.96. Lastly, the factor correlation equals 0.62. The high correlation lends credence to the claim that these two factors depend on a higher-order factor, which I confirmed.

So far, I have focused on the GSS measures in one data set. Note that I observe the same pattern of results in other GSS cross-sectional surveys. Since I rely on data from four ANES surveys, it would help to see if the observed GSS results replicate in an ANES cross-section. Since most of these

---

[17] Given ordinal data, I again applied the categorical ULS estimator to the polychoric correlation matrix.

[18] The good fit is not due to having a model with one degree of freedom. When I respecify the model so that same-sex relations and elective abortions load on one factor and traumatic abortions and gay marriage load on the second factor, the model chi-square = 174.93 (p <0.001), NNFI = −0.60, SRMR = 0.10, and RMSEA = 0.80.

Table 4 A CFA model for abortion and gay rights
items, 2006 GSS non-Black respondents

	Estimates
ξ_1 Abortion	
λ_1 Traumatic abortions	1.00
	0.92
λ_2 Elective abortions	0.99
	0.91
ξ_2 Gay rights	
λ_3 Homosexuality wrong	1.00
	0.96
λ_4 Gay marriage	0.85
	0.81
Factor correlation	0.62
Model fit:	
Satorra-Bentler corrected χ^2 / 1 df	0.79
χ^2 p value	0.37
NNFI	0.97
SRMR	0.004
RMSEA	0.12
Number of observations	1,471

Robust categorical ULS estimates based on polychoric
correlations. Unstandardized factor loadings reported, with
standardized loadings in italics. All parameter estimates are
significant at $p < 0.01$.

contain a single abortion item, I can't specify a two-factor model. Fortunately,
the 2012 ANES survey has eight abortion questions and four gay rights items.

The abortion items tap into traumatic and elective circumstances. The gay
rights items cover antidiscrimination laws, military service, gay marriage, and
gay adoption. Table 5 reports the correlation matrix from the 2012 ANES cross-
section.[19] Once again, each correlation is positive, many are strong, and none
are weak. They range from 0.34 to 0.85. As one would expect, the traumatic–
elective abortion pair (0.65) and the gay marriage–gay adoption pair (0.85) are

---

[19] The matrix includes polychoric and polyserial correlations.

Table 5 A correlation matrix for abortion and gay rights items, 2012 ANES non-Black respondents

	Traumatic abortions	Elective abortions	Gay marriage	Gays adopt children	Anti-gay discrimination	Gays armed forces
Traumatic abortions	1.00					
Elective abortions	0.65	1.00				
Gay marriage	0.46	0.48	1.00			
Gays adopt children	0.46	0.50	0.85	1.00		
Anti-gay discrimination	0.36	0.37	0.67	0.65	1.00	
Gays armed forces	0.34	0.35	0.64	0.64	0.64	1.00

Notes: All correlations significant at $p < 0.01$. The table reports polychoric and polyserial r correlations. Mean correlation $= 0.53$. Number of cases equals 2,048.

among the highest. The mean pairwise correlation equals 0.53. Clearly, people take consistent positions in response to this varied set of items.

To see if these responses derive from a common source, I applied the CFA method to the ANES correlation matrix. Once more, a two-factor model reproduced the matrix better than the one-factor model.[20] Table 6 shows that model fit is strong across the board; the factor loadings are high; and the interfactor correlation comes in at 0.63 – matching what we saw in the GSS data. This high correlation indicates that both factors depend on a higher-order factor – that is, on a common attitudinal disposition.

Stepping back, the key takeaway here is that people respond to the abortion and gay rights items in a consistent manner. Some people habitually take conservative positions on these issues. They oppose abortion and equal rights for LGBT individuals. Others usually respond in a progressive way. Far more often than not, they favor reproductive rights and same-sex rights. The correlation and measurement modeling estimates suggest that the responses people give to all the items spring from a common attitudinal disposition.

In my judgment, this pattern of results justifies combining the abortion and gay rights items into a simple additive scale. While this move violates the practice of combining items that derive from a single factor into a scale, I believe it is a reasonable move for three reasons. First, people who favor/oppose abortion typically favor/oppose equal rights for gays and lesbians to an impressive degree. Second, a single moral issues scale is more parsimonious than distinct abortion and gay rights scales. Third, the moral issue scale is also more reliable than two separate scales.

2.3 Scale Reliabilities

So far, I have shown two things. First, the standard measures of parenting values that appear on the ANES and the GSS surveys tap into the same latent variable – authoritarianism. Second, the abortion and gay rights items derive from two closely related latent variables. These factors correlate at 0.62 in the GSS and 0.63 in the ANES. This in turn suggests that a single higher-order attitudinal disposition guides the responses people give to all of the abortion and gay rights items. In short, the available items are valid indicators of latent moral issue attitudes. These items do a good job of homing in on the underlying construct. I therefore sum up the answers people give and take their average response to calculate their moral issue scores.

---

[20] The model includes a correlated error term between the "job discrimination" and "armed forces" items.

Table 6 A CFA model for moral issues, 2012 ANES
non-Black respondents

	Estimates
ξ_1 Abortion	
λ_1 Traumatic abortions	1.00
	0.78
λ_2 Elective abortions	1.06
	0.83
ξ_2 Gay rights	
λ_3 Marriage	1.00
	0.93
λ_4 Adoption	1.00
	0.93
λ_5 Protection from discrimination	0.77
	0.71
λ_6 Gays in the armed forces	0.74
	0.69
Factor correlation	0.63
Model fit:	
Satorra-Bentler corrected χ^2 / 7 df	0.46
χ^2 p value	0.98
NNFI	1.00
SRMR	0.004
RMSEA	0.00
Number of observations	2,048

Notes: Robust categorical ULS estimates are based on
polychoric correlations. Unstandardized factor loadings
reported, with standardized loadings in italics. All
parameter estimates are significant at $p < 0.01$. The
model includes a correlated error term between the
"protection from discrimination" and the "gays in the armed
forces" items.

Readers will no doubt wonder how reliable these scales are. Quite reliable as
it turns out. Table 7 reports the ordinal alpha reliability coefficients for each
multi-item scale on the first wave of each panel data set I use. Each cell in the
table gives two numbers: the alpha reliability value and the number of items in

Table 7 Ordinal alpha reliability coefficients for the moral issues and parenting scales, non-Black respondents

	Moral issues (all items)	**Moral issues (2 items)**	**Parenting values (all items)**
GSS 2006	0.96 / 9	0.75 / 2	0.68 / 2
GSS 2008	0.96 / 9	0.78 / 2	0.70 / 2
GSS 2010	0.96 / 9	0.73 / 2	0.69 / 2
Mean	0.96	0.75	0.69
ANES 1992	0.79 / 4	0.52 / 2	0.80 / 4
ANES 2000	0.70 / 3	0.45 / 2	0.83 / 4
ANES 2012	0.93 / 12	0.73 / 2	0.78 / 4
ANES 2016	0.83 / 4	0.73 / 2	0.80 / 4
Mean	0.81	0.61	0.80
Grand mean	0.88	0.67	0.75

Notes: The first number in each cell is the ordinal alpha reliability coefficient. The second number is the number of items used to construct the scale. Number of observations ranges from 343 to 2,357.

a given scale.[21] The first column of data shows the reliability of the moral issues scales based on all available items. The next column reports the reliability for a two-item scale that uses one abortion item and one gay rights item that appear on both panel waves.[22] Section 3 explains why I use two-item scales. For now, just note that it lets me probe the robustness of some of the results I obtain using the longer scales. The last column reports the alpha coefficient for the child-rearing scales.

Here are the take-home points. First, the reliability of the full-item moral issues scales ranges from acceptable to good in the three-to-four-item ANES scales (0.70–0.83). It is excellent in the nine-item GSS scales (0.96) and in the twelve-item ANES scale (0.93). The mean reliability for moral issues comes in at 0.88 across the seven panels. Second, reliability drops for the two-item moral issues scales. The estimates range from a low of 0.45 in the 2000 ANES to a high of 0.78 in the 2008 GSS. That said, most of the two-items scales exceed 0.70, and the

---

[21] Ordinal alpha uses tetrachoric and polychoric correlations that reflect the categorical nature of these variables (see Zumbo et al. 2007).

[22] For these scales I use the broadest abortion question and the gay marriage question, whenever the latter was available.

mean reliability comes in at 0.67. This is a little lower than the recommended 0.70 cutoff, but not much. Third, the reliability for the child-rearing scale varies from 0.68 to 0.70 in the GSS to 0.78 to 0.83 in the ANES – solid values all. Overall, the mean reliability is 0.75.

In conclusion, the full moral issues scales are highly reliable on average, and the authoritarianism scales are less reliable on average, but still respectable. This gap is larger in the GSS surveys than the ANES surveys. I return to this point later in the Element.

2.4 Summary

This section has served two purposes. First, prior research has relied on the workhorse child-rearing questions in the ANESs and, to a far lesser extent, on the fairly similar items in the GSSs. Some have assumed that the responses people give to both sets of items come from the same source. Others have harbored doubts. With new data from a 2020 YouGov survey, I found that the ANES and the GSS items correlate robustly and load on a single latent factor. Hence, we can treat the ANES and GSS items as comparable measures of latent authoritarianism. This implies that the same results should emerge when using the ANES and the GSS scales as dependent or independent variables in multivariate models. This is basically what I find in Sections 3–5.

My second purpose in this section has been to demonstrate that survey responses to standard abortion and gay rights questions derive from a common attitudinal impulse. These items do a good job tapping into latent attitudes toward moral issues. The CFA evidence showed that a two-factor model does a better job fitting the data than a one-factor model, but the interfactor correlation is high enough (0.62–0.63) to package these items together into additive scales. This is the path I take moving forward.

3 Moral Issue Attitudes Are More Stable Than Authoritarianism

This section takes up the stability of moral issues and authoritarianism. The common view is that parenting values are more stable than policy views. How do we make comparisons like this? Social scientists employ an array of different methods to gauge stability. A popular approach is calculating the correlation between the answers participants give to the same survey question/s at two points in time. Continuity correlations tell us whether the positions people take on some matter are consistent from one reading to the next. The greater the number of respondents who respond in a consistent way over time, the higher the correlation will be. If everyone in the sample took the same position at time$_1$ and time$_2$ or, failing that, maintained the same position in the distribution, the correlation would equal 1.00. If everyone responded randomly to these questions both times, the correlation would be about 0.00. Again, higher correlations denote more stability.

We can also look at the percentage of respondents who fall on the same side of some divide at two points in time. Those who do are "stand patters." To illustrate, folks who are very liberal on some controversy at $time_1$ and only slightly liberal at $time_2$ have stood pat. The strength of their views may vary, but they remain liberal. They count as stable. If everybody remains on the same side of their divide over time, the stand patters will be 100 percent. Conversely, if everyone switches sides, with some moving from liberal to conservative and others moving in the opposite direction, the percentage of "switchers" will be 100 percent. Sections 3.2 and 3.3 compare the stability of fixed/fluid values and moral issue attitudes using both of these methods. But first I offer some brief comments on the panel data I introduced in Section 2.

3.1 Panel Data Sources

I rely on data from seven panel studies. Four of these serve as workhorse data sets throughout this Element; they are the 2016–2020 ANES panel and three GSS panels, which span the 2006–2010, 2008–2012, and 2010–2014 periods. These four panels contain $time_1$ and $time_2$ measures of moral issues and child-rearing values. In addition, I use data from the 1992–1996 ANES panel, the 2000–2004 ANES panel, and the 2012–2013 ANES recontact study. The first two measured moral issues in both waves and child-rearing values in the first wave. The recontact study measured child-rearing values in both waves and moral issues in the 2012 wave. These three panels let me assess the stability of one construct in a given survey.

Some final comments about data quality. The ANES and the GSS surveys employ best practices in survey design, sampling methods, and weight construction to yield representative national samples of the voting-age public. Spanning three decades of the American political experience, the data let me assess stability over the history of the culture war. Last, there is a lot of variability in the questions I employ to measure parenting values and moral issues. As I showed in Section 2, these disparate sets of items serve as valid and reliable measures of their respective latent constructs. This is a design strength. A consistent pattern of results will mean that the inferences I draw do not depend on this or that set of measures.

3.2 Continuity Correlation Tests

I begin with the most widely used method of testing for attitude stability. Table 8 reports the Pearson r correlations for the moral issues and authoritarianism scales across the seven panels. Recall that only four of the seven panels have

Table 8 Continuity correlations for moral issues and parenting values, non-Black respondents

	Moral issues (all items)	**Moral issues (two items)**	**Parenting values**
GSS 2006–2010	0.83 / 9	0.77 / 2	0.54 / 2
GSS 2008–2012	0.84 / 9	0.78 / 2	0.52 / 2
GSS 2010–2014	0.85 / 9	0.77 / 2	0.58 / 2
NES 1996–1996	0.80 / 4	0.70 / 2	–
NES 2000–2004	0.74 / 3	0.67 / 2	–
NES 2012–2013	–	–	0.66 / 4
NES 2016–2020	0.77 / 4	0.74 / 2	0.61 / 4
Mean	0.81	0.74	0.58

Notes: The first number in each cell is the Pearson r correlation. The second number is the number of items used to construct the scale. Number of observations ranges from 343 to 2,357.

measures of both constructs in both waves. For moral issues, I report the correlations for scales made up of all the items on the survey. I then do the same for the two-item scales. Recall that the latter include one abortion and one same-sex item.[23]

What is the point of employing a two-item moral issues scale? My use of abbreviated scales serves two purposes. In Section 2, I showed that the moral issues scales are more reliable on average than the child-rearing scales (see Table 7). This difference is most pronounced in the GSS data (mean $\alpha = 0.96$ for issues and 0.69 for values). With the two-item moral issues scales I hold scale length constant to provide a more direct "apples to apples" comparison of moral issue and value stability in the GSS data. If the two-item moral issue scale is as stable as or more stable than the two-item authoritarianism scale in the GSS, we cannot attribute the difference to the number of items in the moral issues scale. Instead, it would seem that moral issues really are more stable than child-rearing values.

The second reason I use two-item moral issues scales is to stack the deck against the moral issues stability hypothesis in the ANES data sets. If responses to the two-item moral issues scales are more stable than responses to the four-item parenting values scale, moral issues will have passed a hard test. This is

---

[23] For the GSS data, I use the "abortion if the woman wants it for any reason" and "sexual relations between two adults of the same sex" items. For the ANES data, I use the standard four-point abortion item and the position on gay marriage item, when available. When the latter is not, I use the protection from discrimination item. See the online appendix for the full wording.

because the two-item moral issues scales are less reliable on average than the child-rearing scales (0.61 < 0.80).

On to the analysis. Table 8 contains the results, again for all non-Black respondents. To begin with the full moral issues scale, the correlations span a fairly narrow range. The lowest estimate sits at 0.74 in the 2000–2004 ANES. The highest estimate comes in at 0.85 in the 2010–2014 GSS. The ANES correlations lag the GSS correlations a bit, but the key point is that all of them are quite high. The mean correlation across the six panels equals 0.81. By the standards used to judge attitude stability, these correlations are high relative to what we often see for issues. These values are impressive in light of the four-year gaps that separate $wave_1$ from $wave_2$ in each panel.

In column 2, we see that the two-item moral issues scales are less stable than the full-item scales in every panel – exactly what we would expect when we drop items. What is, in my estimation, most notable is how small the drop-offs are. The mean continuity correlation for the full-item scales is 0.81. The two-item analogue is 0.74, suggesting that on average Americans hold crystallized attitudes about abortion and gay rights.

Let's focus on the GSS estimates. For the nine-item scales, the average correlation is 0.84. The average for the two-item scale is nearly as high at 0.77. In the latter case, the positions people take on whether women should have the right to choose "for any reason" and "sexual relations between two adults" hold very steady – as steady, in fact, as the seven-point measure of party ID (mean continuity correlation = 0.79). The mean stability for the two-item ANES scales is also very solid (0.70), if not quite as high as its GSS counterpart. In sum, whether we employ longer or shorter scales does not make much of a difference. The positions people take on moral issues in the present are very consistent with the positions they took four years ago (also see Goren and Chapp 2024).

Next up, let's see how stable the child-rearing scales are. The third column in Table 8 reveals middling values that range from 0.52 to 0.66. The mean stability is 0.55 in the GSS and 0.64 in the ANES. The highest correlation (0.66) is from the 2012–2013 ANES, which, readers should remember, spans eight months. These values are not as high as we usually find for other predispositions such as party ID and religiosity (Goren and Chapp 2017; Kinder and Kalmoe 2017).

The theory of authoritarian judgment presumes that fixed/fluid values outlast moral issue attitudes. The theory of moral power asserts that moral issue attitudes are as durable as core predispositions. When I compare the correlations, moral issues eclipse authoritarianism in every single test. Let's look at the means. The full-item moral issues scales are more stable than the parenting values across all studies (0.81 > 0.58), in the GSS studies (0.84 > 0.55), and in the ANES studies (0.77 > 0.64). The two-item moral issues scale also proves more stable in all panels (0.74 > 0.58), in the GSS panels (0.78 > 0.55), and in the ANES panels (0.70 > 0.64). The latter result is quite informative. It reveals that the responses people give to a simple two-item moral issues scale persist longer than the responses they give to the ANES four-item parenting scale. Moreover, the moral issues stabilities come from three four-year panels, while the parenting stabilities come from a four-year panel and an eight-month panel. Even with the deck stacked firmly against the moral issues stability hypothesis, moral issues prove more durable than authoritarianism.

No matter how I slice the data, the same conclusion emerges. Across disparate data sets and sets of measures, the feelings people hold toward abortion/gay rights last longer than their beliefs about conformity, obedience, autonomy, and the like. These results are compelling, but incomplete because they cannot tell us who remains loyal to their side. In light of this, I undertake a second set of response stability tests.

3.3 A Second Test: Stand Patters and Switchers

In this section, I focus on how many people remain on the same side of the divide and how many people switch positions over time. Those who remain true are "stand patters." Those who move are "switchers." Let me illustrate this with an example. Think about someone today who is pro-life and anti-gay. If she disapproves of abortion and gay rights four years later, we conclude that her views are stable. The intensity of her opinion may wax or wane over time, but this doesn't matter. What matters is that she stays put in the same camp. She stands pat. Now think about a different person who endorses fluid values like autonomy, independence, and diversity. If four years later he embraces fixed values like conformity, obedience, and uniformity, he has switched sides. He has moved from the libertarian camp to the authoritarian camp – he's a switcher.

With panel data, it is a simple matter to isolate those who stand pat and those who switch. I tabulate the answers subjects gave to the questions in both waves and tally up how many stayed versus how many strayed. I rely on data from the four panels that contain measures of both constructs at time$_1$ and time$_2$. For moral issues, I again use the full-item scale and the two-item scale. Those who were progressive both times, moderate both times (i.e., at the scale midpoint), or conservative both times count as stand patters. Likewise, those who endorsed fixed values both times, fluid values both times, or who fell squarely in the middle count as stable. Table 9 has the results.

The top row in the table lists the percentage of the public that remained in the same moral camp – whether progressive, moderate, or conservative – in each

Table 9 Stand patters and switchers on moral issues and parenting values, non-Black respondents

| | Percentage stable | | | | |
	GSS 2006–10	GSS 2008–12	GSS 2010–14	ANES 2016–20	Mean
Moral issues (all items)	82	85	83	85	84
Moral issues (2 items)	73	73	72	82	75
Parenting values	73	78	80	63	74

Notes: For moral issues, cell entries represent the percentage of respondents who took consistent positions on moral issues over time (i.e., progressive both waves, moderate both waves, or conservative both waves). For parenting values, percentage stable represents the percentage of respondents who took consistent positions on values over time (i.e., authoritarian both waves, moderate both waves, or libertarian both waves).

panel. For the full-item scale, some 82–85 percent of respondents took consistent positions on abortion/gay rights in both waves. This works out to a mean of 84 percent – an impressive value.[24] To put it differently, more than eight in ten Americans stood pat on moral issues for periods lasting four years.

Turning to the second row, I find somewhat lower values for the two-item moral issues scale. Here, my estimates suggest that 73–82 percent of the American electorate stood pat on moral issues. The mean is 75 percent – three in four Americans. These, too, are impressive figures. In conjunction with the full-scale results, the data make it plain that public opinion on moral issues is very stable. Most people stay on the same side of this issue divide over time. Moral progressives do not waver in their commitment to reproductive rights and rights for same-sex individuals. Moral conservatives remain steadfastly opposed.

Do most people stay on the same side of the authoritarian–libertarian divide? The data in row 3 show that the answer is a conditional yes. In the GSS panels, 73–80 percent of respondents stood pat. However, in the 2016–2020 ANES panel, this number dropped to 63 percent. Why the difference? It is not due to differences in scale reliability. Table 7 from Section 2 shows that the ANES scale is more reliable than the GSS scales (0.80 > 0.69). The answer likely has something to do with the rise of Donald Trump. Perhaps the drumbeat of authoritarian appeals he made persuaded millions of Americans, who already

---

[24] The comparable figure for the seven-point party ID scale (leaners counted as partisans) is 77 percent.

liked him for other reasons, to draw closer to him on this divide (compare with Lenz 2012).

In any case, the mean percentage of stand patters is 74 percent. This is on par with the 75 percent average for the two-item moral issues scale, but it lags behind the 84 percent average we see for the full-item scale. Simply put, large swaths of the American public also stood pat on beliefs about the trade-offs between fixed and fluid values that constitute the authoritarian cleavage. This is an important finding. Just as important is the result that moral issues are more crystallized – at least when we look at the better measure of opinion on abortion/ LGBT rights. These results reinforce the continuity correlations in Table 8. By both metrics, moral issue attitudes prove more stable than fixed/fluid values. Authoritarianism does endure over time. But the visceral feelings people harbor toward abortion and gays last even longer.

3.4 Summary

This section has examined how durable authoritarianism and moral issues are in the minds of voting-age Americans. Data from seven panel studies that cover the past three decades of political experience converge on a simple conclusion. Moral issues hold steadier and fluctuate less than authoritarianism in the minds of most people. These results support the claim that moral issue attitudes are stronger than authoritarianism. They dent the claim that the latter functions as a worldview that holds belief systems together. If it did, one would expect it to wobble less than views of the issues that it presumably constrains. But this is just a small dent, a single piece of evidence against the "authoritarianism-as-crowning-posture" claim.

If high stability is a necessary condition for designation as a core predisposition, moral issues may have a case. But stability alone cannot sustain such a claim. We need more evidence to sustain the proposition that moral issue attitudes are strong. We need evidence of impact. Sections 4 and 5 provide that evidence.

4 Moral Issue Attitudes Are More Impactful Than Authoritarianism I

In one perspective, authoritarianism functions as a crowning posture – a worldview – in mass belief systems. This psychological force emerges early in the life cycle, endures for long stretches of time, repels the influence of other idea elements, and impacts political judgment and behavior. This reasoning underlies the causal ordering laid out in model (a) of Figure 1. In the standard model, authoritarianism shapes party ID, moral issues, and candidate evaluations. Its effects manifest throughout the belief system. By contrast, the theory of moral power contends that attitudes toward abortion and gay rights are also strong. They persist over time. They are hard to move. They induce change in core predispositions. This reasoning underlies the alternative model (b) laid out in Figure 1. In this model, moral issue attitudes act as a crowning posture. They induce partisan and value change when predispositions are misaligned with issues.

Section 3 established that moral issues are more durable than fixed/fluid values. This is consistent with the claim that moral issue attitudes are stronger than these values, but it does not speak directly to the question of what causes what. In this section, I bring evidence to bear on this question. If moral issue attitudes are as strong as my theory claims, then they should predict change in authoritarian/libertarian values. In what follows, I rely heavily on cross-lagged regression techniques as detailed in Section 4.1. This method is better at approximating causal dynamics than methods that rely on cross-sectional data. Even so, the method is not foolproof. It cannot deliver definitive causal estimates. Hence, I deploy other techniques to test the values-to-issues and issues-to-values hypotheses. No matter what approach I take, the results are always the same. Moral issues repeatedly predict change in authoritarianism. Authoritarianism rarely predicts moral issue change. This evidence is consistent with the theoretical claim that moral issues are stronger than authoritarianism. The results imply, but cannot prove, that views of abortion/gay rights function more like a crowning posture than authoritarian values.

4.1 Modeling Strategy

Value-centric theories of political judgment hold that abstract normative beliefs shape the positions people take on the issues of the day. The theory of moral power asserts that attitudes toward abortion/same-sex rights shape basic predispositions, including core values. To date, most of the evidence that backs the parenting-values-over-issues hypothesis rests on cross-sectional data analysis (e.g., Hetherington and Weiler 2009; Cizmar at al. 2014). With such data, analysts assume that fixed/fluid values guide the positions people take on moral issues rather than the reverse. They cannot test the validity of this causal assumption.

To get at questions like this, scholars turn to panel data. Adopting this approach, recent work explores whether parenting values predict change in political judgments or the reverse. Here, the limited evidence is mixed. Luttig (2021) used data from a Survey Sampling International panel during the 2016 election season and from the 2012–2013 ANES. He used cross-lagged regressions to model the dynamic relationship between partisan attitudes and the standard child-rearing scale. He measured partisan attitudes with feeling thermometers for the Republican Party (both panels), Donald Trump (2016), and Mitt Romney (2012). The results did not confirm the authoritarianism-as-worldview prediction on two counts. First, the parenting values scale did not predict change in partisan attitudes in any model. Second, partisan attitudes did predict change in parenting values in three of four tests.

Next, Bakker et al. (2021) relied on data from the three GSS panels to test for two-way relationships between conformity/autonomy values and an array of political judgments. They found evidence of two-way relationships. Fixed/fluid values induced change in abortion opinion, LGBT opinion, and liberal–conservative ID, but not party ID. At the same time, opinion on both issues and ideology predicted value change, but party ID did not.

In a third study, Engelhardt et al. (2023) used data from two panel studies to test if fixed/fluid values change in response to other political attitudes and beliefs. They looked at data from the 2012–2013 ANES survey and a 2017–2018 YouGov panel. Like Luttig (2021), Engelhardt et al. (2023) also used cross-lagged models. In contrast to Luttig (2021), Engelhardt et al. (2023) corrected for RME in the estimates. Across nine models, they showed that neither social (e.g., religiosity) nor political (e.g., party ID, Trump feelings) variables predicted change in child-rearing values. This, of course, supports the standard view. They did not test whether the child-rearing scale predicts change in political views over time.[25]

Overall, these disparate results frustrate efforts to draw firm conclusions. Bakker et al. (2021) uncovered some support for the authoritarianism-to-political-outcomes pathway. Luttig (2021) found no support, and Engelhardt et al. (2023) did not test for it. Bakker et al. (2021) and Luttig (2021) showed that authoritarianism is endogenous to political variables, but Engelhardt et al. (2023) found no such thing. It is hard to know what to make of these differences. The studies use different measures of fixed/fluid values; look at different political outcomes; rely on different data sets; specify different models; and deploy different estimators. The results suggest that authoritarianism may be endogenous to some political judgment, but the evidence is limited in scope.[26]

---

[25] In other tests, they used cross-sectional data to show that the usual four-item and a modified eight-item child-rearing scale predict a range of outcome variables. The eight-item scale did a better job on this score.

[26] In a non-US study, Smith et al. (2021) drew on data from a five-wave panel carried out during the 2018 Brazilian presidential election to see if parenting values evolved over the course of the campaign. As called for by the standard view, authoritarian leanings at the start of the campaign predicted later support for the authoritarian candidate, Jair Bolsonaro. But prior opposition to

To test the competing claims (in the context of a single issue-area), I rely on a much larger set of panel studies and deploy a wider range of techniques. As we saw in Section 2, the GSS and ANES measures of parenting values tap into latent authoritarianism to a similar degree. This provides the justification needed to rely on the measures from both sources. Furthermore, I estimate cross-lagged regression models that do not correct for RME and cross-lagged models that do. The use of error correction techniques is controversial. Some maintain that RME in survey responses reflects weak, uncrystallized attitudes and beliefs in the public mind (Converse 1970; Zaller 1992). Others hold that RME is largely attributable to faulty questions rather than weak attitudes, thereby justifying error corrections (Goren 2004). I take no position on this here. Instead, my goal is to provide a full suite of estimates to satisfy readers from both camps. Finally, I use the fixed effects estimator to test for within-person change in issues and values (Allison 2009).

To start, I use the cross-lagged regression model to test the values-to-issues and issues-to-values hypotheses in seven panel data sets. Researchers employ these models to unpack the dynamic relationship between predispositions and issues. The setup looks like this.

$$\text{Moral Issues}_t = \beta_1 \text{Moral Issues}_{t-1} + \beta_2 \text{Authortarianism}_{t-1} + Z_{t-1} + e_{1t} \quad (1)$$

$$\text{Authoritarianism}_t = \beta_3 \text{Authortarianism}_{t-1} + \beta_4 \text{Moral issues}_{t-1} + Z_{t-1} + e_{2t} \quad (2)$$

Note that β_1 and β_3 summarize the predicted impact that the lagged dependent variables at time t−1 (i.e., the first wave of the panel) have on the dependent variables at time t (i.e., the second wave). Further, β_1 represents the stability of moral issues over time. It estimates the variation in moral issues$_t$ explained by issues$_{t-1}$, holding authoritarianism$_{t-1}$ and the lagged covariates (symbolized by Z_{t-1}) constant. Then, β_3 captures the stability of authoritarianism, all else equal. Insofar as moral issues and authoritarianism endure, these coefficients will be statistically significant and large.

The cross-lagged coefficients β_2 and β_4 are the key quantities of interest. In these equations, β_2 captures the effect of lagged authoritarianism on current issues, controlling for lagged issues and the other covariates, β_4 is the predicted effect moral issues$_{t-1}$ has on authoritarianism$_t$, holding this lagged predisposition and all else constant.[27] All models control for multiple social demographic variables and party ID. The key variables range from zero to one. This scaling

---

Bolsonaro predicted subsequent movement in the anti-authoritarian direction on parenting values. This contradicts the authoritarianism-as-crowning-posture model.

[27] The e_{1t} and e_{2t} symbols represent the error terms in the respective equations. These terms capture the effect of omitted variables on both orientations along with inherent randomness in human preferences.

lets us interpret the cross-lagged estimates as percentage changes on the outcome variables.[28] Lastly, I use ordinary least squares (OLS) regression, which ignores RME, and errors-in-variables regression (EIV), which accounts for RME.[29]

4.2 Results

To keep things simple, I take three steps. First, I rely on forest plots to present the key quantities of interest – that is, the OLS and EIV estimates of the cross-lagged coefficients β_2 and β_4 in Equations (1) and (2). Second, I confine the complete set of OLS and EIV estimates to the online appendix (see Tables A1–A4). Interested readers can peruse these at their leisure. Third, I utilize a pair of statistical graphics to compare the substantive impact that parenting values have on moral issues and the reverse moral-issues-to-values effects.

4.2.1 Moral Issues Shape Authoritarianism Far More Than the Reverse

Figure 2 reports the results of the authoritarianism-to-moral-issues tests among non-Black respondents. For these tests, I can use data from six of the seven panels. The top forest plot presents the OLS point estimate summarizing the predicted impact authoritarianism$_{t-1}$ has on moral issues$_t$, controlling for lagged issues, lagged party ID, and the social demographic variables in each data set. The plot at the bottom covers the EIV estimates. Each circle represents the point estimate of β_2. The lines that extend out from each circle are the lower- and upper-95 percent confidence limits. The mean effect (θ) and 95% confidence intervals (CIs) appear at the bottom of each forest plot. What does support for the authoritarianism-as-crowning-posture theory look like? It looks like this: positive point estimates and the lower confidence limit lying to the right of the 0.00 reference line that extends up from the x-axis.

Let's start with the OLS estimates in the top pane. The results lend limited support for the conventional theory. On the plus side, every coefficient is positive. All else equal, those fully committed to fixed values at time$_{t-1}$ subsequently oppose abortion and gay rights to a greater degree than those committed to fluid values. The biggest effect emerges in the 2010–2014 GSS. There, anti-abortion/ anti-gay sentiment rose by 7 percent among authoritarians relative to

---

[28] Note that the variables vary to a similar degree across the full range of values. In the ANES data sets, the parenting scale always evinces more variation than the moral issues scale (standard deviations, 0.31 > 0.27). The pattern flips in the GSS panels as the moral issues scale varies a bit more than the values scale (0.32 > 0.28). Note also that nontrivial percentages of respondents take the minimum or maximum value on each variable in each panel study. This means that the percentage interpretations for the point estimates do not overstate the practical impact that one variable has on the other. Hence, we can use the estimates to make meaningful comparisons and draw reasonable conclusions.

[29] The reliability estimates in Table 7 serve as inputs into the EIV models.

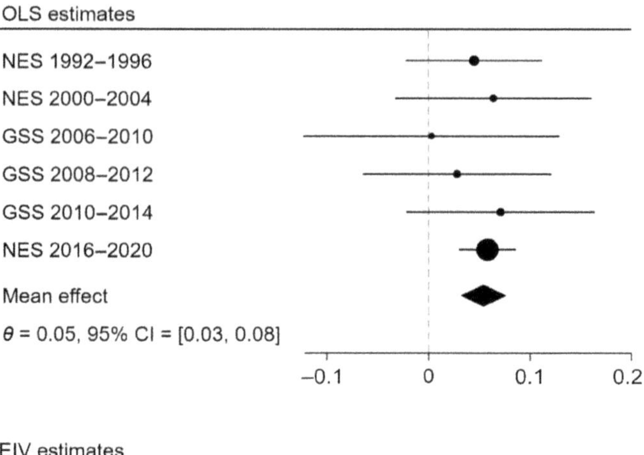

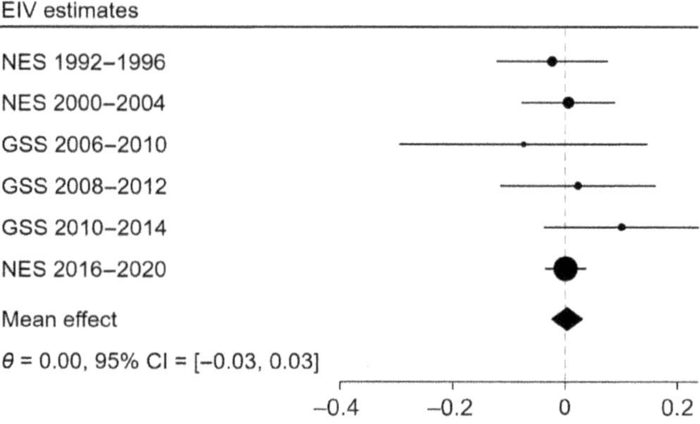

Figure 2 A forest plot summarizing the effects of authoritarianism$_{t-1}$ on moral issues$_t$, showing OLS and EIV estimates.

Notes: Each point estimate comes from the cross-lagged model reported (online) in Tables A1 (OLS in the top plot) and A2 (EIV in the bottom plot). The point estimate for each study is bounded by 95% CIs. The mean effect θ represents the precision-weighted point estimate across all six data sets. I also report the 95% CI for θ. The weight of each study is proportional to the size of the point estimate circle.

nonauthoritarians – a decent sized effect ($p < 0.10$). The other effects are smaller, ranging from just over 0 percent in 2006–2010 to 6 percent in 2016–2020 ($p < 0.001$). All of this is consistent with the standard view. But, on the minus side, five of the six effects do not differ significantly from zero. The only exception occurs in the 2016–2020 ANES panel. By this point in time, authoritarianism had come to predict opinion change. Between 2016 and 2020, the gap on moral issues between those who prioritized fixed values and those who prioritized fluid values grew by 6 percent.

What is the average effect across the data sets? To get the average OLS effect, I use meta-analysis. This method weighs the point estimate from each study by its precision to calculate the mean effect in the six studies. The more statistically precise a given estimate, the greater its weight in calculating the mean effect. The bottom row reveals a mean effect of 0.05 (symbolized by the diamond shape in the forest plot). The 95% CI equals [0.03, 0.08]. This is a real, if rather small, effect. On average, those who fully endorsed authoritarian values in the first wave became 5 percent more conservative on abortion/same-sex rights in the second wave compared to those who rejected these values. The effect does not emerge consistently across the individual panels; it emerges only in the pooled data driven largely by the NES 2016–2020 study. An equivocal result, to be sure.

Moreover, OLS estimates do not correct for measurement error. Some readers may prefer estimates that remove RME from the observed variables. When I turn to the EIV estimates in Figure 2's bottom pane, the evidence is unequivocal. When RME is removed, the limited support for the authoritarianism-to-moral-issues hypothesis vanishes. Study-specific estimates hover around zero. Some are positive. Others are negative. Outside of the 0.10 effect in the 2010–2014 GSS ($p < 0.10$), every effect is incorrectly signed and/or tiny. Most critically, the point estimate is not reliably distinguishable from zero in any data set. No surprise, then, to see that the mean EIV effect $\theta = 0.00$. The 95% CI is [−0.03, 0.03].

To sum up, the conventional take on the power of authoritarianism to structure issue positions fares quite poorly in the case of abortion and equal rights for gays and lesbians. Across all OLS and EIV models, the parenting scale predicts issue change beyond chance levels in one of twelve tests (the 2016–2020 OLS model). The mean effect across the six OLS models proves significant beyond chance levels but modest in terms of real-world impact. On average, authoritarians score 5 percent more conservative on moral issues down the line compared to libertarians. The mean EIV effect is 0.00 and statistically insignificant. Now, it may well be that authoritarianism structures positions on other issues, but that does not appear to be the case for abortion and gay rights.

Let's see how the moral-issues-to-authoritarianism prediction fares. Here, the available data permit tests in five of the seven panels.[30] Figure 3 reports the β_4 estimates in the OLS models (top pane) and the EIV models (bottom pane) along with the 95% CIs. If the theory of moral power is not wide of the mark, we should observe positive coefficients with lower confidence

---

[30] Because the 1992–1996 and the 2000–2004 ANES panels lack time$_2$ measures of parenting values, I cannot test this prediction.

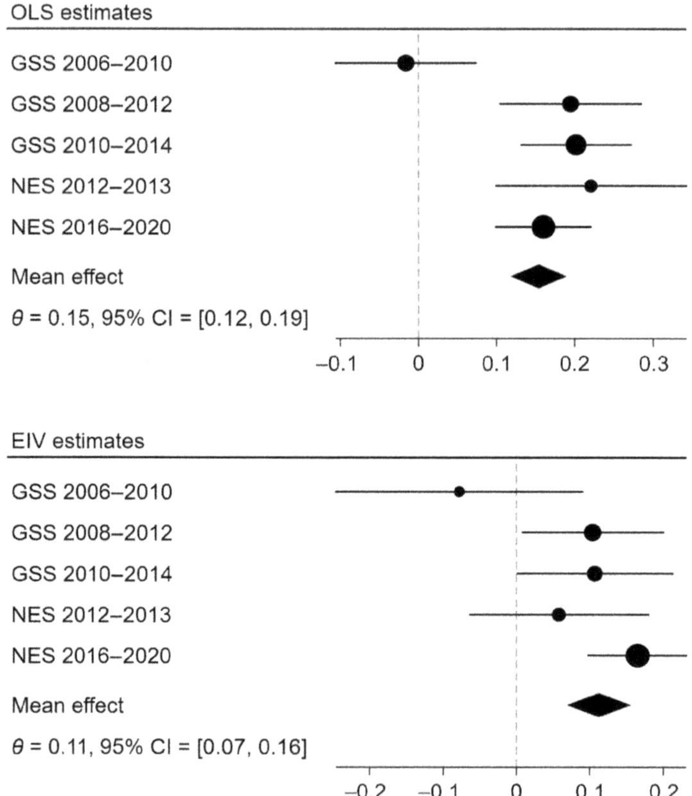

Figure 3 A forest plot summarizing the effects of moral issues $_{t-1}$ on authoritarianism$_t$, showing OLS and EIV estimates.

Notes: Each point estimate comes from the cross-lagged model reported in Tables A3 (OLS in the top plot) and A4 (EIV in the bottom plot). The point estimate for each study is bounded by 95% CIs. The mean effect θ represents the precision-weighted point estimate across all six data sets. I also report the 95% CI for θ. The weight of each study is proportional to the size of the point estimate circle.

limits to the right of the 0.00 reference line. Since the general pattern of results is similar across the OLS and EIV models, I discuss them jointly.

Here are the takeaway points. First, Figure 3 shows that lagged moral issues have the correct sign in eight of the ten models – all but the 2006–2010 GSS. Next, the issue scale predicts parenting value change in seven of the ten models. Significant effects emerge in four of the five OLS tests and three of the five EIV tests (all $p < 0.05$). Third, while the magnitude varies from study to study, the issue effects mostly lie in the 10–20 percent range. When cognitive dissonance arises, many people seem to resolve it by adjusting their core beliefs to fit their feelings about abortion and gays.

Here are some examples. Those who took the most conservative stance on abortion and gay rights in 2016 grew 16 percent stricter on child-rearing values in 2020 compared to those who were the most progressive on the issues. This holds true in both the OLS and the EIV equations. Next, in the OLS models the distance between moral conservatives and progressives on parenting values grew by about 20 percent from 2008 to 2012 and then again from 2010 to 2014. In the EIV models, the comparable estimates are 10 and 11 percent – smaller but still respectable. The predicted effects weaken because the error corrections render the child-rearing scale more stable, and thus harder to move. That said, moral issues still engender change in authoritarianism.[31]

With respect to the mean effects, here is what I observe: OLS $\theta = 0.15$, 95% CI = [0.12, 0.19] and EIV $\theta = 0.11$, 95% CI = [0.07, 0.16]. These means denote substantial 15 percent and 11 percent effect sizes, respectively. The bottom line is clear. The positions people take on abortion and LGBT rights systematically, reliably, and robustly predict change in their views on how best to raise children. Authoritarianism is, in other words, endogenous to moral issues.

I will now compare the impacts authoritarianism and moral issues have on one another. There are a couple of different ways to do this. First, I simply evaluate the mean effect sizes. In the OLS models, the mean-issue-to-fixed /fluid-value effect is 0.15. The mean-value-to-issue effect is one-third of this at 0.05. And since the respective 95% CIs do not overlap ([0.12, 0.19] vs. [0.03, 0.08]), we can conclude that this difference is statistically real – it is not a chance difference. I draw the same inference from the EIV estimates. The issue-to-value effect is larger substantively (0.11 > 0.00) and statistically (95% CIs = [0.07, 0.16] and [−0.03, 0.03]), respectively. These differences underscore the main takeaways from this section. Moral issue attitudes usually structure authoritarianism. Authoritarianism rarely structures moral issue attitudes.

The second way to underscore these differences is with a simple statistical graphic. The plots in Figures 5–6 accomplish this goal. Each figure displays the predicted linear effect that authoritarianism (on the x-axis) has on moral issue opinions (on the y-axis) in the plot on the left, and the reverse effect of issues (now on the x-axis) on authoritarianism (now on the y-axis) in the plot to the right. My plots are based on the OLS estimates. Figure 4 is for the 2008–2012 GSS. Figure 5 covers the 2016–2020 ANES. Keep in mind that these models control for the lagged dependent variable, lagged party ID, and demographics. The OLS coefficient, along with its t-score, appears in the lower right-hand corner in each graphic to give readers a quick summary.

---

[31] The biggest gap between the OLS and the EIV models happens in the 2012–2013 ANES. The effect is large and highly significant in the OLS model (0.22, $p < 0.01$), modest and insignificant in the EIV model (0.06).

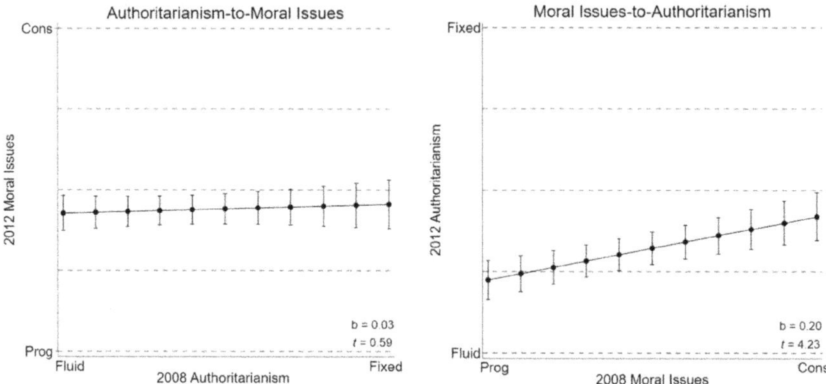

Figure 4 The impact of authoritarianism/moral issues on moral issues/
authoritarianism, 2008–2012 GSS non-Black respondents.

Notes: Point estimates bounded by 95% CIs. Estimates derived from the OLS models
reported in Tables A1 and A3.

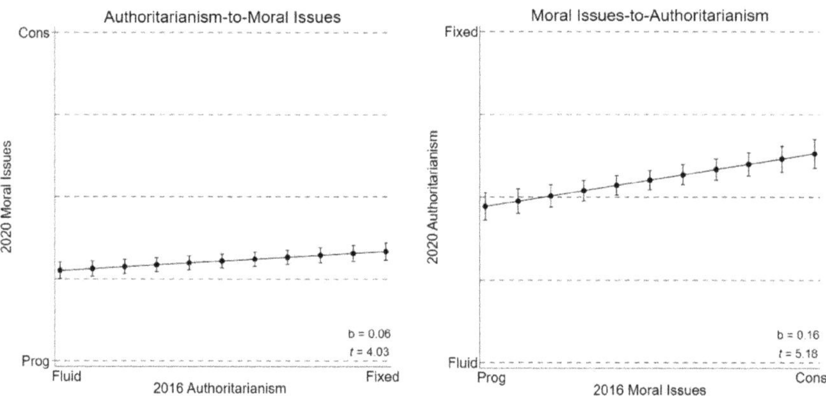

Figure 5 The impact of authoritarianism/moral issues on moral issues/
authoritarianism, 2016–2020 ANES non-Black respondents.

Notes: Point estimates bounded by 95% CIs. Estimates derived from the OLS models
reported in Tables A1 and A3.

Figure 4 gives us the fixed/fluid values-to-issue effect to the left. In the 2008–
2012 GSS, we see that authoritarianism does not predict change in moral issue
positions over time. The flat regression slope makes this clear. The most
authoritarian respondents (i.e., at the fixed end of the x-axis) in 2008 scored
3 percent more conservative on moral issues in 2012 versus the most libertarian
respondents (i.e., at the fluid end of the scale) in 2008. No difference at all.

But when we turn to the plot to the right, the picture is much different. That plot shows that moral issues predict substantial change in fixed/fluid values over time. As we go from the progressive to the conservative end of the issue scale in 2008, subjects shifted 20 percent closer to fixed or stricter parenting values in 2012. Put another way, the gap on authoritarianism between the most pro-choice/pro-gay and the most anti-abortion/anti-gay folks rose by 20 percent in four years ($p < 0.001$).[32]

Figure 5 illustrates the 2016–2020 ANES results. The authoritarianism-to-moral-issues plot reveals a statistically meaningful though substantively modest effect. Here, we find that parenting values predict change in moral issue positions down the line. The most ardent authoritarians in 2016 scored 6 percent more conservative on moral issues in 2020 relative to the most ardent libertarians in 2016 ($p < 0.001$). This is the only data that supports the authoritarian structuring hypothesis. The fact that this is the lone confirmation I found in twelve tests puts this effect in context. It is an outlier. It is the exception to the rule in the period 1992–2020. It may signify that something fundamentally changed when Trump came to power, or it may be an effect unique to Trump. What happens after he exits the political arena remains to be seen.

Why does the effect emerge only in the Trump years? One possibility is that Trump's persona and messaging primed the authoritarian disposition more frequently and intensely than any of his GOP predecessors, thereby facilitating stronger linkages between it and related policy attitudes. The other possibility is that the increased precision resulting from the much larger sample size in this data set ($n = 2,132$) makes it easier to detect authoritarianism's modest effect. Recall that the magnitude here (0.06) is comparable to that in three of the other five data sets.

In any case, the plot to the right shows that the predicted impact of moral issues on authoritarianism is, once again, much bigger than the reverse. Those who disapproved of abortion and same-sex rights in 2016 scored 16 percent more authoritarian on the parenting values scale in 2020 compared to 2016's most pro-choice, pro-gay respondents ($p < 0.001$).[33] This effect is similar in magnitude to what we see in most of the other data sets.

The last several pages have covered a lot of statistical ground. I now take a step back and consider the big picture, the bottom-line conclusions I can draw from the wealth of data. The main conclusions are clear. The evidence comes down decisively in favor of the theory of moral power and lends almost no support for the authoritarianism-as-worldview theory – at least, on this

---

[32] The difference between the issues-to-parenting values and the values-to-issues slopes is significant (0.20 > 0.03, $p < 0.001$).

[33] The issue-to-parenting effect is stronger than the value-to-issue effect (0.16 > 0.06, $p < 0.01$).

particular pair of issues. With respect to the authoritarianism-to-moral-issues hypothesis, I have found that parenting values predict moral issue change in only one of twelve tests and that the effects range from negligible to modest. With respect to the moral-issues-to-authoritarianism hypothesis, my results show that moral issues predict dispositional change in seven of ten tests; the mean issue effect is 0.15 in the OLS models and 0.11 in the EIV models (both $p < 0.001$); most of the study-specific effects are fairly substantial; and the mean issue-to-values effects are much stronger than the values-to-issues effects in the OLS models ($0.15 > 0.05$, $p < 0.01$) and EIV models ($0.11 > 0.00$, $p < 0.01$). Moral issue attitudes, in short, are much stronger than authoritarianism.

4.2.2 Where Does Party ID Fit In?

In total, every piece of evidence suggests that the gut-level feelings people harbor toward abortion and gay rights last longer, more readily repel influence, and carry greater impact than authoritarianism. These findings have emerged in multiple data sets covering thirty years of political experience, for varied measures of both constructs, and no matter how I treat RME. Moral issue attitudes really seem more durable and impactful than authoritarianism.

Does this mean that authoritarianism is weak? In my view, this conclusion is unwarranted at this time. There are two reasons for this. First, readers should recall that I controlled for party ID in the models predicting change in fixed/fluid values. Tables A3 and A4 in the online appendix show that the coefficient for the party ID is never correctly signed and significant in these models. In plain language, party ID does not systematically affect the endorsement or rejection of fixed parenting values. This finding is consistent with some of the work I cited earlier (Bakker et al. 2021; Englehardt et al. 2023).[34] The resilience of authoritarianism vis-à-vis partisan influence attests to its strength. It does not bend in response to what many scholars regard as the core predisposition in the public mind. Second, it remains unclear if other issues move authoritarianism. Maybe they do, maybe they don't. More work is needed to find out.

Of course, none of this undercuts the theory of moral power. Authoritarianism, like party ID, may structure the positions people take on multiple issues and the candidates they back on Election Day. That influence does not extend to structuring the positions people take on abortion and gay rights. Instead, the direction of influence seems to run from moral issues to authoritarianism. When these sit in tension, moral issues drive the subsequent resolution.

---

[34] Note that GOP ID predicts moral issue conservatism in two of twelve models, suggesting limited party-to-issue effects when parenting values are held constant (see Tables A1–A2).

4.2.3 Alternative Explanations

As with all observational data, alternative explanations abound. To reassure readers that the inferences I have drawn about the strength of moral issues are not fragile, I estimated some alternative models to show that the issue variable effect holds. I did two things here. First, Lenz and Sahn (2020) have shown that in many published studies the key theoretical variables achieve significance only when control variables enter the model. When the model excludes the controls, the key theoretical variables no longer differ significantly from zero. This is known as a suppression effect.[35] To determine if the control variables are artifactually inflating the effect size and the statistical significance of the moral issues variable, I took Lenz and Sahn's (2020) advice to drop all the control variables (except lagged parenting values) and reran the models. The results did not change, which means that the predicted effect moral issues have on authoritarianism is not the byproduct of misleading suppression effects.

Second, omitted variable bias poses another obvious threat to the inferences I have drawn about the impact of moral issues. To guard against this threat, I used data from one GSS and one ANES survey to probe the robustness of the moral-issues-to-authoritarianism effect. With data from the 2008–2012 GSS, I estimated an OLS model that regressed the parenting value scale on the usual suspects and several additional control variables. These included variables that I believe capture early socialization effects, such as being a rural resident at age sixteen, being a big-city resident at age sixteen, the mother's level of education, and the same for the father. I also controlled for whether the subjects had babies, preteen children, or teenagers at home. The moral issues effect remained significant ($b = 0.11$, $p < 0.05$) in this panel. I then pivoted to the 2016–2020 ANES to run more tests. I controlled for having nonadult children, being a rural resident, being a big-city resident, having a gay family member, having a gay friend, gender conservatism, biblical literalism, religiosity, and openness to experience. Across four different specifications, the moral-issues-to-authoritarianism effect held in every model, albeit in slightly weaker form. Summing up, the impact that moral issues have on authoritarianism seems robust. Readers can find these results in Tables A5 and A6 of the online appendix.

I carried out one final robustness test using the two-period fixed effects (FE) estimator (Allison 2009). This lets me test if within-person change on moral issues predicts within-person change on parenting values. The method's utility

---

[35] Their reanalysis of forty-nine published observational studies yielded a startling finding. In over 30 percent of these studies, the presence of control variables pushed the key explanatory variable from small and insignificant in bivariate models to large and significant in multivariate models.

comes from letting each person in the sample serve as their own control for all covariates that do not vary over time. This applies to both measured and unmeasured variables. Any variable that does not change from wave to wave cannot explain change in some other variable. This rules out many rival explanations. Because of this, the models provide a stronger basis for causal inference than cross-lagged regression models. But since these models cannot rule out other time-varying factors as alternative explanations for parenting value change, I cannot draw a definitive causal inference about the ability of moral issues to induce that change. Hence, in the models presented in Table 10, I control for whether the number of nonadult children living at home changed in the panels. Perhaps having more children leads people to adopt more-conservative parenting values (Lönnqvist et al.2018) and more-conservative positions on abortion and same-sex rights (Stenner 2005).

Table 10 contains the FE estimates.[36] Note that the analysis is confined to the four data sets that have measures of all variables in both waves. To begin with 2006–2010, issue change does not predict change in child-rearing values. The coefficient has the incorrect sign, but it falls short of significance. But since, as we saw earlier, moral issues did not predict values in cross-lagged models, this is not surprising (see Figure 3). For whatever reason, moral issues and authoritarianism did not covary in that period. Next, the estimates from the 2008–2012 GSS behave as called for by the theory of moral power. The moral-issues-to-values effect is both significant ($p < 0.05$) and solid in substantive terms ($b = 0.20$). Subjects who moved in the abortion/gay rights direction came to favor conformity in children over thinking for themselves. The final GSS estimate tells a similar story, albeit one with a lot of uncertainty. A rightward shift in opinion on moral issues predicts a rightward shift on values ($b = 0.10$.) The magnitude of the effect, though solid, is imprecise ($p = 0.25$). The final column in Table 10 has the ANES result. Here, moral issue change predicts authoritarianism change once more. The effect is real ($b = 0.12$) and significant ($p < 0.01$). A meta-analysis returns an average effect size of 0.09 across the four panels, with a 95% CI = [0.02, 0.16]. There is much variability in these estimates.

---

[36] To measure within-person change, I subtracted each respondent's $time_1$ issue score from their $time_2$ score. The resulting scale ranges from -1 to 1. A score of -1 means that a respondent with the most traditional position on abortion/gay rights in $time_1$ adopted the most progressive position on these issues at $time_2$. A score of 1 means that a subject who took the strongest pro-abortion/pro-gay stances at $time_1$ switched to the strongest anti-abortion and anti-gay rights positions at $time_2$. A score of 0 denotes no change (i.e., an individual held the same position both years). I used the same procedure to calculate how much individuals changed on authoritarianism. Here, a score of -1 reflects maximum movement in the libertarian direction while a score of 1 is maximum movement in the authoritarian direction.

Table 10 An OLS model of within-person change
in authoritarianism over time

	GSS 2006–10	GSS 2008–12	GSS 2010–14	ANES 2016–20
Moral issue Δ	−0.11	0.20[*]	0.10	0.12[**]
	(−1.27)	(2.19)	(1.17)	(2.59)
Had more children Δ	0.00	−0.00	0.01	0.00
	(0.23)	(−0.16)	(0.43)	(0.24)
Constant	0.03	−0.01	−0.03	−0.03[**]
	(1.58)	(−0.38)	(−1.96)	(−3.52)
Number cases	157	334	301	2,124

[*]$p < 0.05$ (two-tailed test).
Notes: Unstandardized coefficients reported with t-values in parentheses. Estimates adjusted to account for the complex sample design. Each coefficient estimates the degree to which within-person change in moral issues from time 1 to time 2 predicts within-person change in authoritarianism.

Overall, the takeaway should be clear. The various robustness tests reinforce my main finding. Moral issue attitudes really do seem to drive change in the authoritarian disposition. In test after test after test, feelings about abortion/gay rights shape a core predisposition long presumed to lie beyond the reach of such feelings. At this point, I can say that the results are consistent with the claim that moral issues operate more like a crowning posture than parenting values. But, again, I cannot draw a definitive causal inference from the observational data on which I have relied.

4.3 Summary

Many political psychologists have theorized that authoritarianism is a foundational element – a crowning posture – in the minds of individual voters. In this perspective, it structures the stances people adopt on political issues; the parties they identify with; and who they vote for (Stenner 2005; Barker and Tinnick 2006; Hetherington and Weiler 2009). Furthermore, it eludes the reach of political judgments. Because authoritarianism is both exogeneous to – and has wide-ranging influence on – the political judgments that citizens make, the claim that it serves as a worldview seems sensible. By extension, the inference that authoritarianism drives political conflict and polarization in American politics also seems plausible.

The work done in Sections 3 and 4 indicates that a note of caution is in order. There is no doubt that authoritarianism and moral issues are associated in the public mind, but it is not because the former structures the latter. Instead, the exact opposite appears to be the case. Moral issue attitudes persist longer than authoritarianism; resist the influence of authoritarianism; and induce change in authoritarianism. Moral issue attitudes are stronger than the authoritarian disposition.

But what of the claim that authoritarianism functions like a worldview? Do the results reported here undercut that claim? My results do not furnish a definitive answer to that question. I have not conducted an exhaustive inquiry on whether fixed/fluid values shape or depend on other political attitudes and beliefs. On the one hand, it seems likely that parenting values affect public opinion on national security issues – issues that are probably too distant from daily living for many people to develop strong feelings about. On the other hand, it also seems possible that attitudes toward immigration may be strong enough to drive change in fixed/fluid values (see Abrajano and Hajnal 2015). The need for additional work could not be clearer.

One thing I can do in the pages that remain is to try to unpack the relationship between moral issues, authoritarianism, and party ID. Doing so sheds more light on the relative power of moral issues and authoritarianism. As noted earlier, the estimates reported in Tables A3–A4 show that authoritarianism resists the influence of party, which speaks to its power and buttresses the conventional wisdom (compare with Englehardt et al. 2023). Moral issues may also shape party ID to a much greater extent than the reverse (Goren and Chapp 2017, 2024). But what remains unsettled is how authoritarianism affects party ID relative to moral issues. If parenting values manifest stronger effects than issues, the authoritarianism-as-worldview theory receives critical support. But if the reverse pattern holds, if moral issues manifest much stronger effects over party ID, the theory of moral power gains credence. Section 5 explores these dynamics in detail.

5 Moral Issue Attitudes Are More Impactful Than Authoritarianism II

In Sections 3 and 4, I showed that attitudes toward abortion and gay rights are more durable than core beliefs about conformity, autonomy, order, and related values; that these values do not routinely shape these attitudes; and that moral issues constrain these values to a surprising degree. All of this points to an elementary conclusion: moral issue attitudes are more powerful than authoritarianism. These findings strongly imply that moral issue attitudes play a more central role in the political mind of the public than authoritarianism, that some issues are stronger than some predispositions. In this section, I put this claim to another round of tests.

I do so by modeling the relationship between moral issues, child-rearing values, and party ID. One influential perspective holds that authoritarianism became "an important determinant of party identification in the early twenty-first century" (Hetherington and Weiler 2009, 7). If this is the case, we can infer that authoritarianism structures party conflict in the mass public. We can further infer that clashes between authoritarian worldviews fuel conflict in the broader electoral and party systems.

To preview where this section ends up, I find that when we take moral issues into account, there is little support for the claim that authoritarianism structures party ID. Instead, moral issues play the more prominent role. My analysis of cross-sectional data from the 1992–2020 ANESs reveals that moral issues have shaped party ties throughout this period; that authoritarianism had no effect until 2016; and that the effects of moral issues on party ID are 350 percent larger on average than the effects of authoritarianism during this era. Next, my analysis of panel data shows that moral issues routinely induced partisan change; that authoritarianism did not do so until 2016; and that the effect of moral issues surpasses that of authoritarianism by an average of 500 percent. These results buttress the claim that moral issues play a major role in structuring US political conflict – far more than currently recognized. The role authoritarianism plays pales in comparison.

5.1 Predicting Party ID: Cross-Sectional Analyses

A number of theories posit that party ID functions as a prime mover of political attitudes, beliefs, and perceptions (see Johnston 2006 for a review). But this position is not universally shared (e.g., Abramowitz and Saunders 1998). In fact, both the theory of authoritarianism and the theory of moral power contest it. Hetherington and Weiler (2009) and Feldman and Weber (2023) make the case that authoritarianism structures party ID. Goren and Chapp (2017, 2024) argue that feelings about abortion and gay rights structure party ties. If either factor shapes party ID more so than the reverse, then two important conclusions follow. First, the argument for the centrality of that factor in mass belief systems grows stronger. Second, the case that the factor plays a central role in driving system-level conflict becomes more tenable.

As a first step to gain some empirical leverage on these questions, I use cross-sectional data to regress party ID on moral issues, fixed/fluid values, and a set of covariates. This lets me gauge the relative impacts that moral issues and fixed/

fluid values have had on party ID throughout the history of the culture war. Now, some readers might object that I've got the party-issue relationship backwards, that party ID is a cause of moral issue attitudes, not a consequence. While a reasonable supposition, it has not fared well in some recent work. As I noted earlier, Christopher Chapp and I (Goren and Chapp 2017, 2024) have tested the party-ID-to-moral-issues and moral-issues-to-party-ID hypotheses. In seven different panel data sets, the effects of issues on party ID were more than twice as large – and often much larger – than the party-to-issue effects.[37] In short, this recent evidence suggests that moral issues systematically affect party ID to a much greater extent than the reverse. This provides some justification for modeling party ID as a function of moral issues.

A couple of additional points before I dive into the analyses. To begin, this is obviously an exploratory exercise. The estimates I generate cannot fully isolate the relative impact that these factors have on party ID. The panel data evidence indicates that the party-issue relationship is bidirectional. To be clear, the moral-issues-to-party effect is much stronger than the party-to-moral-issues effect, but the latter effect is not negligible in some of the models. Hence, the moral-issues-to-party-ID effects I report here reflect some upward bias. At the same time, these estimates ignore the indirect effects that moral issues have over party ID via the moral-issues-to-authoritarianism link established in Section 4. This downwardly biases the estimated moral-issues-to-party effect. Whether these biases offset is not clear. My goal here is simply to provide a rough cut at how well these factors predict party ID. If the statistical association is much higher for moral issues relative to fixed/fluid values, we learn something important about the theories of moral power and authoritarianism. We learn that moral issues are more impactful, that they matter more to voters and to politics.

Second, while it may seem to some that this is a simple question of "horse race" empirics, I must stress that this is not the case. If authoritarianism and moral issues predict party ID to a similar degree, both variables have a fair claim to function as central organizing elements in mass belief systems. But if the effects of one variable greatly outpace the other, the results speak to what voters really care about and how their concerns affect American politics. Such results

---

[37] We used these data sets (Goren and Chapp 2024): (1) 1992–1996 ANES; (2) 2000–2004 ANES; (3) 2006–2010 GSS; (4) 2008–2012 GSS; (5) 2010–2014 GSS; (6) 2006–2012 Portrait of American Life Survey; and (7) 2016–2020 ANES. In a series of cross-lagged OLS regression models, the mean effect of issues on party ID was 0.15 (95% CI = [0.13, 0.17]). The mean effect of party ID on issues was 0.07 (95% CI = [0.06, 0.09]). When we reran the models using EIV regression, the results came down even more decisively in favor of moral issues. Here, the mean moral-issues-to-party-ID effect was 0.11 (95% CI = [0.08, 0.13]). The mean party-to-moral-issues effect was an incorrectly signed and substantively trivial −0.03 (95% CI = [−0.01, −0.04]).

can also shed light on how candidates should campaign when aiming to build a minimal winning coalition.

I use data from the ANES cumulative file. The four-item child-rearing scale shows up on the 1992, 2000, 2004, 2008, 2012, 2016, and 2020 surveys (ordinal alpha = 0.80 across the surveys). I tap into moral issues with three items. These include the four-point abortion scale; a four-point scale that asks if subjects support or oppose laws that ban discrimination against gays and lesbians; and a yes/no question on support for gay/lesbian adoption (ordinal alpha = 0.75). The online appendix has the question wording. I measure party ID using the standard seven-point scale.

I estimate two sets of models to predict party ID. The first model includes two predictors: parenting values and moral issues. I call this the "two-variable" model. The second model controls for a number of other predictors of party ID. The multivariate model adds these covariates:

- Hispanic self-identification (dummy variable)
- Age (measured in years)
- Woman (dummy variable)
- Married (dummy variable)
- College graduate (dummy variable)
- three income dummy variables (Middle, Upper, Wealthy)
- Southern resident (dummy variable)
- Church attendance (three-point scale)
- Biblical literalism (dummy variable)
- Religious importance (dummy variable).

Why include the two-variable model? I do so because it provides a very simple and direct way to assess the robustness of each predictor. As discussed in Section 4, Lenz and Sahn (2020) have shown that when analysts add control variables to statistical models, the effect size and significance of the key theoretical variable often rises. Again, this is called a "suppression effect." Whenever the key findings depend on suppression effects, we can conclude that such results are not robust. If the key explanatory variable predicts the dependent variable in a multivariate model but not the bivariate model, we usually have grounds to doubt its impact. Lenz and Sahn (2020) recommend that researchers report the results of simpler model specifications. This is what I do in the two-variable model.

I estimate the two-variable and multivariate models in the seven cross-sections listed just now, which means there are fourteen sets of estimates. This is too much data to present in tabular form, so I use a coefficient plot to relay the key quantities of interest. Readers who want to see the full suite of results should check out the online appendix (Tables A7–A9).

Figure 6 contains the results. Let me break down what it tells us about the relative impacts that the child-rearing and moral issues scales have on party ID from 1992 to 2020. First, the plot to the left reports the key estimates from the two-variable models. The plot to the right does the same for the multivariate models. Second, each point is an OLS coefficient, bounded by its 95% CI. The predicted effects that authoritarianism has on party ID appear in the top half of each plot. The coefficients for the moral-issues-to-party-ID effect appear in the bottom part of the plots. Third, the numbers atop the point are the specific OLS estimates. Given the coding of the variables, I expect positive coefficients.[38] And since all variables lie on a zero-to-one scale, we can interpret these as percentage changes. Last, note that the dashed vertical reference line crosses the x-axis at 0.00. When a confidence interval crosses this line, we conclude that the variable in question may not significantly affect party ID that year.

A quick example should make things clear. Take a look at the third point in the authoritarianism pane in the two-variable plot. We see that $b = 0.04$. This means that in 2004 the most authoritarian respondents were 4 percent closer to the GOP than the most libertarian respondents, holding moral issues constant. Because the 95% CI crosses the 0.00 reference line, we cannot conclude that this is a statistically meaningful effect. In plain language, we cannot conclude with a standard level of confidence that authoritarianism predicted party ID in 2004, holding moral issues constant. Now, turn to the analogous estimate in the multivariate model plot on the right. Here, we see that the 2004 OLS coefficient for authoritarianism has risen to 0.12. This means that strong authoritarians were 12 percent closer to the GOP than strong libertarians, holding moral issues and all else constant. Also, the 95% CI no longer passes over the 0.00 reference line. So, when the control variables laid out earlier enter the model, authoritarianism's effect on party ID increases by 300 percent and now achieves significance. Since the coefficient achieves significance in the multivariate model but not the two-variable model, I conclude that the effect of authoritarianism on party ID in 2004 is fragile. It emerges in one model but not the other.

With the stage set, I proceed to the full set of results. The lede is that moral issues consistently and powerfully predicted party ID while authoritarianism failed to have any effect until Trump showed up. To break this down, I start with the child-rearing estimates in the pre-Trump years. The estimates from the two-variable models reveal incorrectly signed or insignificant effects from 1992 through 2012. The coefficient hovers near zero most of the time – sometimes

---

[38] Higher scores denote more support for fixed values; more-conservative moral issue positions; and stronger ties to the GOP.

a little above it (e.g., 2004 and 2012), sometimes below zero (e.g.,1992, 2000, and 2008). The estimate symbolized by the triangle captures the mean effect from 1992 to 2012 – the pre-Trump era. At −0.02, the effect is neither correctly signed nor meaningful in terms of practical impact. It is also insignificant ($p =$ 0.15, two-tailed test).

In the right plot, authoritarianism performs a bit better. When I add control variables to the baseline model, authoritarianism's effect size grows in every data set and now reaches significance twice in the pre-Trump years. First, the effect rises from 0.04 to 0.12 in 2004 and from 0.02 to 0.06 in 2012 ($p < 0.05$ both years). The 2004 OLS estimate means that authoritarians leaned 12 percent closer to the Republican Party than nonauthoritarians, holding moral issues and everything else constant. The 2012 estimate tells us that authoritarians were 6 percent closer to the GOP than nonauthoritarians, all else equal. But, again, the lack of significant effects in the two-variable models indicates that we must be cautious here. The conclusion that authoritarians gravitated toward the GOP in these years is contingent on the presence of a particular group of covariates. Note lastly that the mean authoritarianism effect from 1992 to 2012 comes in at 0.04 ($p < 0.001$).

How do moral issues fare in the time before Trump? Much better, according to the bottom plots in Figure 6. Since the size of the OLS coefficient varies little between the two-variable and multivariate models, it seems fair to conclude that its impact on party ID is indeed robust. The authoritarianism variable seems to have benefited from suppression effects in 2004 and 2012. By contrast, the moral issue variable never depends on the presence of the same control variables to reach significance.

In the multivariate model results, the moral issue effect ranges from a low of 0.32 in 2000 to a high of 0.43 in 2012. The effect is very large and highly significant every year. Here's a specific example. The 2000 estimate tells us that the most zealous pro-life/anti-gay Americans leaned 32 percent closer to the GOP than the most committed pro-choice/pro-gay Americans. Overall, the mean estimate from the pre-Trump years sits at 0.37 – more than nine times the size of the corresponding 0.04 effect for authoritarianism. From 1992 to 2012, the moral issue effect outpaces the child-rearing effect by a factor of three to thirty-five. These are astonishing differences.[39] They imply that moral issues shape party ID far more broadly and deeply than authoritarianism.

---

[39] Recall that the key variables lie on a zero-to-one range, which means that each point estimate in Figure 6 captures the effect that movement across the full range of a given predictor has on party ID. The comparisons I undertake here can be misleading if there is a lot more dispersion on one variable relative to the other. I offer the following assurances that these comparisons do not overstate the moral issues effect versus the authoritarian effect. First, from 1992 to 2020 the mean standard deviation equals 0.31 for issues and 0.32 for the parenting scale. The tiny difference is significant ($p < 0.001$), but with over 17,000 cases this is neither surprising nor

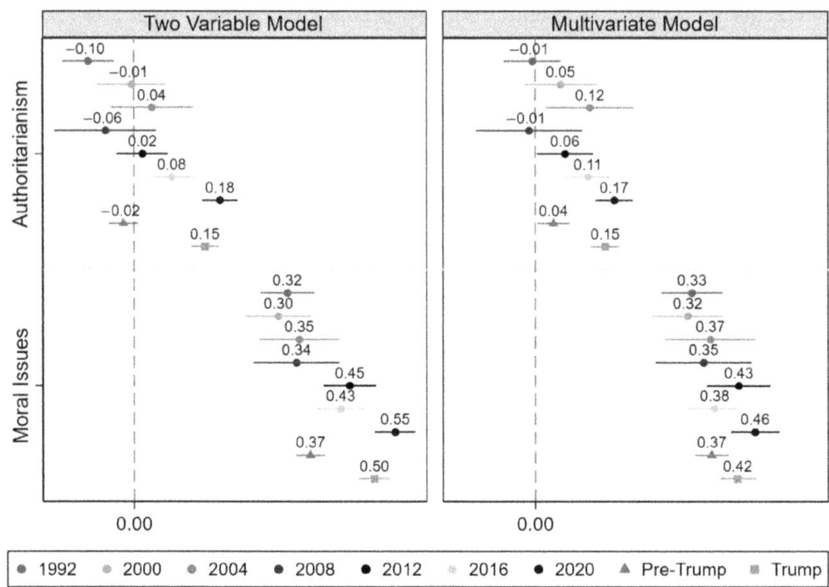

Figure 6 The effects of authoritarianism and moral issues on party ID, 1992–2020 ANES cross-sectional estimates.

Notes: Each point estimate represents an OLS coefficient for the effect a given predictor has on party ID in a given year. Points are bounded by 95% CIs. I use authoritarianism and moral issues to predict party ID in the two-variable model. The multivariate model adds the controls described in the text to the two-variable model. The pre-Trump and Trump estimates include year dummy variables. The vertical reference line corresponds to $b = 0.00$.

Let me emphasize now what transpired during the Trump years. Figure 6 shows clearly that the predicted impact of authoritarianism on party ID rose over time. It now achieves significance in both sets of models in both years. From 2012 to 2016, the OLS estimate jumps from 0.02 to 0.08 in the two-variable model (the rise approaches significance at $p < 0.10$) and from 0.06 to 0.11 in the multivariate model ($p < 0.22$). Although the increased impact is not statistically significant in the multivariate model, its impact nearly doubled. Authoritarianism's effect jumped again from 2016 to 2020, more than doubling in the two-variable model ($0.18 > 0.08, p < 0.001$) and by some 50 percent in the

alarming. Some years, issues vary significantly more than fixed/fluid values (2000, 2004, 2008). The pattern flips in other years (2016 and 2020). But the broader point is that the level of variation is roughly comparable on these variables. Second, in every survey, nontrivial numbers of people score at zero or one on both variables. Third, the standardized beta coefficient for moral issues = 0.34 and 0.03 for authoritarianism in the pre-Trump years. The respective betas are 0.32 and 0.13 for 2016 and 2020.

multivariate model ($0.17 > 0.11$, $p < 0.07$). Simply put, once Trump's hostile takeover of the GOP was complete, authoritarians started moving into the party.

When I combine the 2016 and 2020 data, the authoritarianism effect comes in at 0.15 in the bivariate and multivariate models (see the point estimates symbolized by the square). This is notably larger than the OLS estimates in the pre-Trump era ($b = -0.02$ in the two-variable model and 0.04 in the multivariate model). The estimate tells us that the most authoritarian scored 15 percent higher on GOP affinity than the least authoritarian, controlling for a range of other things including moral issues. Trump's emergence on the national political scene seems to have rendered the GOP more appealing to authoritarians. Before Trump, the GOP did not readily draw authoritarians into its ranks.

By contrast, moral issues predict party allegiance throughout the entire time series. From 1992 to 2012, the influence of issues proved robust at 0.37 in the two-variable and the multivariate models ($p < 0.001$). The effect held when Trump arrived in 2016 ($b = 0.38$) and ran for reelection in 2020 ($b = 0.46$). The pooled estimate for the Trump years reveals a powerful effect. The most morally conservative Americans were 42 percent closer to the GOP relative to the most progressive Americans. This effect is much larger than the 15 percent effect that we saw for the authoritarianism variable. The difference is also highly significant ($p < 0.001$). Overall, the results tell us that moral issues mattered going back some thirty years, and they mattered a lot in every single election – far more than authoritarianism mattered.

To sum up, the cross-sectional data yield three notable findings. First, moral issues have always shaped party ID whereas authoritarianism has only done so in the past two presidential elections. Second, moral issues have always played a much greater role in structuring party ID than authoritarianism has. This was true in 1992, when Patrick Buchanan declared that the GOP was waging a war against liberals and Democrats and the Clintons, a "war for the soul of America." It remained true in 2020 when Donald Trump fiercely berated the mainstream media, the political establishment, and his myriad opponents, threatening retribution against all who defied him. Third, moral issue conservatives have been sorting into the GOP since the dawn of the 1990s (Goren and Chapp 2024). Authoritarians waited about twenty-five years to follow suit. When it comes to partisan sorting, moral issues have always been much more impactful than authoritarianism.

5.2 Predicting Change in Party ID: Panel Data Analyses

In the work done in Section 5.1, the modeling strategy I used presumes that moral issues and authoritarianism precede party ID in the causal sequence. As noted, Goren and Chapp (2024) provide evidence that the direction of influence runs largely (but not entirely) from issues to party. What about the authoritarianism-to-party link? In Section 4, I reviewed the findings from three studies that address the question (Bakker et al. 2021; Luttig 2021; Engelhardt et al. 2023). There, we saw that the question of whether fixed/fluid values drive party change over time remains unsettled.

To bring new evidence to bear on this puzzle, I return to the panel data sets. I test whether authoritarianism predicts party change over time, controlling for lagged party ties, lagged moral issues, and the other background variables. These models serve a second purpose. They can tell us whether moral issues predict party change when we take parenting values into account. If moral issues do so and authoritarianism comes up short, this will lend further credence to the theory of moral power at the expense of the theory of authoritarianism.

Figure 7 uses two forest plots to summarize two sets of cross-lagged regression estimates. The top plot reports the predicted effect that the lagged child-rearing scale from $wave_1$ has on $wave_2$ party ID with $wave_1$ party, moral issues, and all else held constant. The bottom plot reveals the effect that $wave_1$ moral issues have on $wave_2$ party ID, *ceteris paribus*. The online appendix has the full set of OLS estimates (see Table A10).

The data yield strong support for the theory of moral power and little support for the theory of authoritarianism. Let me start with the latter results. In the first six panels, the lagged child-rearing scale fluctuates around 0.00 and never attains significance. In the 2016–2020 ANES, the coefficient proves significant in both substantive and inferential terms (0.07, $p < 0.001$). This single estimate helps the mean effect attain significance, but the key point to note here is how weak the mean effect actually is ($\theta = 0.03$, 95% CI = [0.01, 0.05]).

The panel data results echo what the cross-sectional data showed. Evidently, authoritarianism did not structure party ID or drive party change during the Clinton, Bush II, and Obama presidencies – that is, for twenty-four years. Whatever effects it may have had on other kinds of political judgment, it seemingly played almost no role in partisan sorting before 2016.

The opposite holds true for moral issues. The bottom plot in Figure 7 shows this clearly. Lagged moral issues predict party change in five of the seven regression equations. The issue variable holds the correct sign in the other two. The significant effects range in magnitude from moderate (0.08 in 2012–2013) to large (0.24 in 1992–1996). Across the seven panels, the mean effect is 0.15. The 95% CI estimate tells us that the most morally conservative Americans moved 12–18 percent closer to the GOP over time relative to the

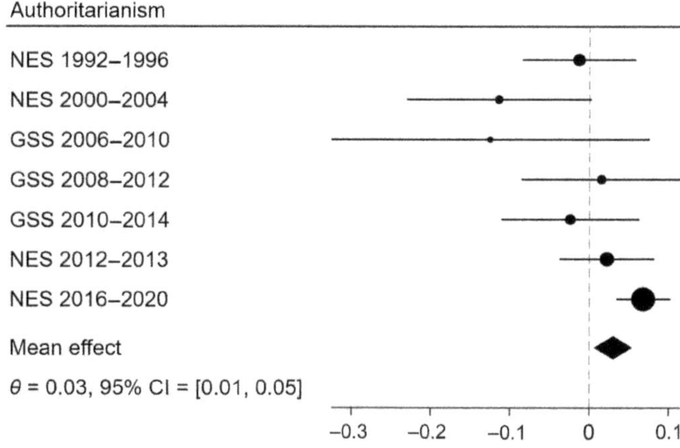

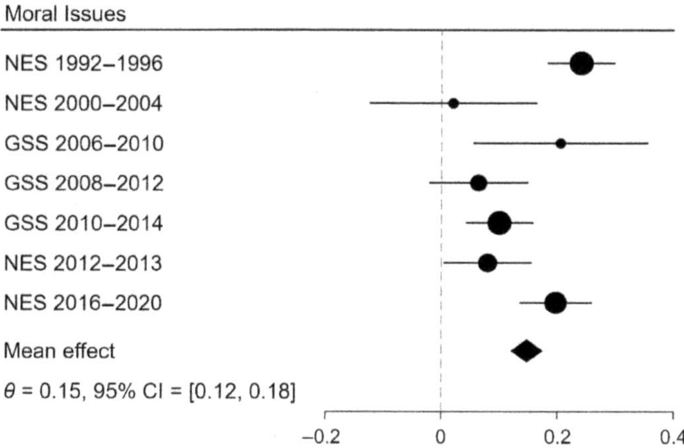

Figure 7 A forest plot summarizing the effects of authoritarianism$_{t-1}$ and moral issues$_{t-1}$ on party ID$_t$, showing OLS estimates.

Notes: The point estimates from the top forest plot come from the cross-lagged model reported in Table A10. The point estimates from the bottom forest plot come from the cross-lagged model reported in Table A11. The point estimate for each study is bounded by 95% CIs. The mean effect θ represents the precision-weighted point estimate across all seven data sets. I also report the 95% CI for θ. The weight of each study is proportional to the size of the point estimate.

most progressive. These results also echo the findings that emerged from my analysis of the ANES cross-sections. For both kinds of data, moral issues guide partisan choice year after year.

Overall, those whose preferences on abortion and gay rights lean conservative have long found the GOP more appealing than the Democratic Party and have sorted accordingly – as early as 1992. In contrast, authoritarians did not begin sorting into the GOP until Donald Trump became the GOP standard-bearer. Over the past three decades, moral sorting has greatly outpaced authoritarian sorting into the parties. As the national parties began to stake out distinct positions on abortion and gay rights in the 1980s and 1990s, voters began selecting into the party that catered to their issue tastes. Their deeper-seated beliefs about conformity, autonomy, and related values played at best a modest role in this process. And even when authoritarian-driven sorting began, issue-driven sorting remained the dominant process.

5.3 Summary

This section has extended the work done in Section 4. There, I showed that feelings about moral issues shape authoritarianism far more than the reverse. Those results provide evidence consistent with the claim that moral issue attitudes are unusually powerful. The results in this section add more weight to this claim. Here, I have shown that moral issues predict party ID more consistently and more robustly than authoritarianism. Two pieces of evidence back this claim.

First, from 1992 to 2020, moral issue opinions have done a much better job predicting party ties than authoritarianism. This holds in every cross-section, in every model, in the pre-Trump years, and in the Trump years. Across the seven cross-sectional surveys, the mean issue effect eclipses the mean authoritarianism effect by 350 percent (0.39 > 0.11). Second, my investigation of panel data arrives at the same verdict. Issues predicted party change in five of seven panels. Parenting values did so only once. Across the panels, the mean effect of moral issues on party ID, holding fixed/fluid values and all else constant, equaled 0.15. This is some 500 percent larger than the mean effect these values had on party change (0.03).

In short, differences between those who support and those who oppose abortion and gay rights have long divided Democrats and Republicans. Differences between authoritarians and nonauthoritarians have been far less central to the party divide. Moreover, the latter differences have only mattered since 2016, and their effects are much weaker than the effects of moral issues. This adds to the growing body of evidence that moral issues are more impact-ful – stronger – than authoritarianism. Section 6 explores what all this means for understanding voters and American politics.

6 Moral Issues Are Stronger Than Authoritarianism and Why It Matters

In this final section, I take stock of the key findings and explain how they inform our broader understanding of American politics. To get things rolling, let's take a look back at the two models diagramed in Figure 1. Model (a) in Figure 1 represents the conventional view, the view that authoritarianism structures party ties, policy positions, and candidate preferences. It functions, in short, as a crowning posture that binds together other elements of political belief systems. As a core predisposition, it persists over time, resists challenge, and shapes political behavior. Because the divisions between those who prefer fixed values and those who prefer fluid values are so intractable and map so directly onto politics, this divide has become the central fault line in American politics (Hetherington and Weiler 2009, 2018).

The theory of moral power situates abortion and gay rights near the apex of mass belief systems. This in turn points to a much different understanding of what propels conflict in the party system and competition in the electoral arena. Model (b) in Figure 1 reflects these differences; it theorizes that gut-level feelings about abortion, gays, and same-sex rights function like a crowning posture in the minds of most Americans. Moral issue attitudes shape partisan affiliation; affect core beliefs about child-rearing; and ultimately motivate voter choice. More simply, moral issue attitudes are durable and impactful – in a word, strong. If this is a reasonable model of how belief systems are organized, we might conclude that abortion/gay rights play a more central role than authoritarianism (and party ID) in driving politics.

The evidence adduced in this Element supports the theory of moral power and fails to support the theory of authoritarian structuring. Section 2 showed that the standard ANES and GSS measures of parenting values tap into the same latent construct. This in turn justified the use of both ANES and GSS data. The fact that the same pattern of results emerged from both sources reinforces my claim that the measures tap into the same construct. Section 3 showed that moral issues are more stable over time than authoritarianism. This was not a function of scale length. When I compared scales made up of equal numbers of items, moral issues proved more durable across the board.

Sections 4 and 5 addressed impact. Section 4 tackled the links between authoritarianism and moral issues. Moral issues proved far stronger than authoritarianism. When mental discomfort arises from conflict between what people believe about the good and just society and how they feel about abortion and gays, they are more likely to resolve this cognitive dissonance by changing their values. Section 5 explored the impact each factor had on party ID. Once more, moral issues eclipsed authoritarianism. And the difference is not close.

All in all, the conclusion that moral issues, not authoritarianism, function as a crowning posture in mass belief systems is hard to avoid. But this claim remains uncertain for at least three reasons. The first reason centers on the simplifying assumptions built into the path models in Figure 1. As I have noted in Section 5.2 and shown elsewhere (Goren and Chapp 2017, 2024), party ID has reciprocal effects on moral issue positions. As a result, Section 5's moral-issues-to-party effects suffer from a degree of upward bias.[40] At the same time, the Section 5 estimates ignore the indirect effects that moral issues have on party via their influence on authoritarianism. This leads to an underestimation of the total effects moral issues have on partisan affiliations. And space limitations prevented me from estimating the relative effects of moral issues, party ID, and authoritarianism on candidate evaluations. Future work will need to sort this out to get better estimates of differences in effect sizes and the nature of these relationships. A second source of uncertainty comes from the measure of authoritarianism. Engelhardt et al. (2023) have developed an expanded eight-item measure of authoritarianism that does a better job predicting other political variables than the four-item measure. If I had been able to use the eight-item scale in lieu of the four-item ANES scale, stronger effects for authoritarianism might have surfaced. This is another question that future research should address.

A third source of uncertainty around the inferences I have drawn revolves around model specification. I have found that the moral-issues-to-authoritarianism effect is robust across several different models, which means that my inferences are not very fragile. That said, the threat of omitted variable bias remains. The relationship between moral issues and authoritarianism may be a spurious by-product of predispositions or issues that do not appear in the model. One issue that comes to mind is immigration. Abrajano and Hajnal (2015) have shown that feelings about immigration are also strong, strong enough to move party ID. Research further shows that immigration attitudes are both durable and grounded in the same kinds of gut-level emotions that underpin attitudes toward abortion and gay rights (Aarøe et al. 2017; Kustov et al. 2021). One might hypothesize that the inclusion of immigration attitudes will greatly dampen the predicted effect moral issues have on authoritarianism and party ID. Fortunately for the theory of moral power, the moral issue effect on both outcomes holds when I include immigration opinion in the respective models.[41] But, since other factors might be at play, this remains an area worthy of close scrutiny.

---

[40] But remember that the moral-issues-to-party influence is much larger than the reverse.

[41] I tested this prediction using data from the 2016–2020 ANES. I tapped into general immigration attitudes with four survey items (V162157, V162158, V162269, and V162270) and added them to the respective panel data models. With $immigration_{16}$ in the model predicting $authoritarianism_{20}$, the moral $issue_{16}$ coefficient declined from 0.16 to 0.14 (both $p < 0.001$). When I did the same thing in the model predicting party ID_{20}, the moral issue variable declined from 0.20 to 0.16 (both $p < 0.001$).

To bring this Element to a close, I share some thoughts on the larger implications my results have for understanding political conflict in the United States. Hetherington and Weiler (2009, 203) argue that authoritarianism has come to play an increasingly central role "in structuring party competition, mass preferences, and the relevant issue agenda of the past forty years. Never since at least the dawning of the survey era has there been such a fundamental clarity and distinction between the two parties on such a wide range of issues organized around a particular worldview."

I agree that the differences between the national parties and their followers on a host of issues are clearer today than in the past. And it is quite plausible that authoritarianism organizes how Americans think about some of these issues. But it does not appear to organize how people think about abortion and gay rights or which political party they choose to affiliate with. On the latter point, the evidence I have assembled in the pages of this Element shows plainly that moral issues structure party ID and party competition more broadly and deeply than authoritarianism.

When George W. Bush campaigned on gay marriage in 2004, he knew that many Americans cared deeply about this issue. He bet that his opposition would motivate many in the GOP base to turn out and vote for him, and that he stood a good chance of getting votes from pro-traditional marriage folks unlikely to support him for other reasons. Given the unpopularity of same-sex marriage back then, he also likely felt that this strategy would grow the size of the GOP coalition. When Donald Trump demonized immigrants in his 2016 White House bid, he sensed that a large swath of the electorate held virulently anti-immigrant views that he believed would help push him to victory. All of this is to say that moral issues and, more speculatively, issues like immigration have fueled political division more readily and far longer than authoritarianism has.

It may be that most people hold weak feelings on most issues, and that most of the time these issues carry little weight in partisan and electoral choice (Lenz 2012; Achen and Bartels 2016; Freeder et al. 2019; but see Ryan 2014). Abortion and gay rights do not fit that profile. They are more durable, less malleable, and more impactful than nearly all other issues. They are even more durable and more impactful than authoritarianism. They have, in short, played a central role in shaping American politics for a long time. In light of the Supreme Court's 2023 *Dobbs* decision to rescind a federal right to abortion; state house and referendum responses in red, blue, and purple states; controversies over "don't say gay" laws; controversies over books and curriculums that cover sexual identity in public schools; and battles over transgender rights, moral issues will continue to play a major role in American politics for many years to come.

References

Aarøe, Lene, Michael Bang Petersen, and Kevin Arceneaux. 2017. "The Behavioral Immune System Shapes Political Intuitions: Why and How Individual Differences in Disgust Sensitivity Underlie Opposition to Immigration." *American Political Science Review* 111(2): 277–294.

Abrajano, Marisa, and Zoltan L. Hajnal. 2015. *White Backlash: Immigration, Race, and American Politics*. Princeton, NJ: Princeton University Press.

Abramowitz, Alan I., and Kyle L. Saunders. 1998. "Ideological Realignment in the U.S. Electorate." *Journal of Politics* 60(3): 634–652.

Achen, Christopher H., and Larry M. Bartels. 2016. *Democracy for Realists: Why Elections Do Not Produce Responsive Government*. Princeton, NJ: Princeton University Press.

Adorno, Theodor W., Else Frenkel-Brunswik, Daniel Levinson, and Nevitt Sanford. 1950. *The Authoritarian Personality*. New York: Harper.

Allison, Paul D. 2009. *Fixed Effects Regression Models*. Los Angeles, CA: Sage.

Altemeyer, Bob. 1981. *Right-Wing Authoritarianism*. Winnipeg: University of Manitoba Press.

Ansolabehere, Stephen, Jonanthan Rodden, and James M. Snyder. 2008. "The Strength of Issues: Using Multiple Measures to Gauge Preference Stability, Ideological Constraint, and Issue Voting." *American Political Science Review* 102(2): 215–232.

Bakker, Bert N., Yphtach Lelkes, and Ariel Malka. 2021. "Reconsidering the Links between Self-Reported Personality Traits and Political Preferences." *American Political Science Review* 115(4): 1482–1498.

Bardi, Anat, and Robin Goodwin. 2011. "The Dual Route to Value Change: Individual Processes and Cultural Moderators." *Journal of Cross-Cultural Psychology* 42(2): 271–287.

Barker, David C., and James D. Tinnick III. 2006. "Competing Visions of Parental Roles and Ideological Constraint." *American Political Science Review* 100(2): 249–263.

Bubeck, Maike, and Wolfgang Bilsky. 2004. "Value Structure at an Early Age." *Swiss Journal of Psychology* 63(1): 31–41.

Bush, George W. 2004. "President Calls for Constitutional Amendment Protecting Marriage." *The White House*, February 24. https://georgewbush-whitehouse.archives.gov/news/releases/2004/02/20040224-2.html.

Campbell, David E., Geoffrey C. Layman, and John C. Green. 2021. *Secular Surge: A New Fault Line in American Politics*. Cambridge: Cambridge University Press.

Carmines, Edward G., and James A. Stimson. 1980. "The Two Faces of Issue Voting." *American Political Science Review* 74(1): 78–91.

Cizmar, Anne M., Geoffrey C. Layman, John McTague, Shanna Pearson-Merkowitz, and Michael Spivey. 2014. "Authoritarianism and American Political Behavior from 1952 to 2008." *Political Research Quarterly* 67(1): 71–83.

Connors, Elizabeth C. 2020. "The Social Dimension of Political Values." *Political Behavior* 42(3): 961–982.

Converse, Philip. 1964. "The Nature of Belief Systems in Mass Publics." In *Ideology and Discontent*, edited by David E. Apter, 206–261. New York: Free Press of Glencoe.

Converse, Philip E. 1970. "Attitudes and Non-attitudes: Continuation of a Dialogue." In *The Quantitative Analysis of Social Problems*, edited by Edward R. Tufte, 168–189. Reading, MA: Addison-Wesley.

Converse, Philip E., and Gregory B. Markus. 1979. *"Plus ça change . . .*: The New CPS Election Study Panel." *American Political Science Review* 73(1): 32–49.

Cook, Elizabeth Adell, Ted G. Jelen, and Clyde Wilcox. 1992. *Between Two Absolutes: Public Opinion and the Politics of Abortion*. Boulder, CO: Westview.

Delli Carpini, Michael X, and Scott Keeter. 1996. *What Americans Know About Politics and Why It Matters*. New Haven, CT: Yale University Press.

Eagly, Alice H., and Shelly Chaiken. 2007. "The Advantages of an Inclusive Definition of Attitude." *Social Cognition* 25(5): 582–602.

Edsall, Thomas B. 2018. "The Contract with Authoritarianism." *New York Times*, April 1. www.nytimes.com/2018/04/05/opinion/trump-authoritarian ism-republicans-contract.html.

Engelhardt, Andrew M., Stanley Feldman, and Marc J. Hetherington. 2023. "Advancing the Measurement of Authoritarianism." *Political Behavior* 45(2): 537–560.

Feldman, Stanley. 1988. "Structure and Consistency in Public Opinion: The Role of Core Beliefs and Values." *American Journal of Political Science* 32(2): 416–440.

Feldman, Stanley. 2003. "Enforcing Social Conformity: A Theory of Authoritarianism." *Political Psychology* 24(1): 41–74.

Feldman, Stanley. 2020. "Authoritarianism, Threat, and Intolerance." In *At the Forefront of Political Psychology: Essays in Honor of John Sullivan*, edited by Eugene Borgida, Christopher M. Federico, and Joanne Miller, 35–54. New York: Routledge.

Feldman, Stanley, and Karen Stenner. 1997. "Perceived Threat and Authoritarianism." *Political Psychology* 18: 741–770.

Feldman, Stanley, and Christopher Weber. 2023. "Authoritarianism and Political Conflict." In *The Oxford Handbook of Political Psychology*, 3rd ed., edited by Leonie Huddy, David O. Sears, Jack S. Levy, and Jennifer Jerit, 733–768. New York: Oxford University Press.

Festinger, Leon. 1957. *A Theory of Cognitive Dissonance*. Stanford, CA: Stanford University Press.

Forero, Carlos G., Alberto Maydeu-Olivares, and David Gallardo-Pujol. 2009. "Factor Analysis with Ordinal Indicators: A Monte Carlo Study Comparing DWLS and ULS Estimation." *Structural Equation Modeling: A Multidisciplinary Journal* 16(4): 625–641.

Fowler, Anthony. 2020. "Partisan Intoxication or Policy Voting?" *Quarterly Journal of Political Science* 15(2): 141–179.

Freeder, Sean, Gabriel S. Lenz, and Shad Turney. 2019. "The Importance of Knowing 'What Goes with What': Reinterpreting the Evidence on Policy Attitude Stability." *Journal of Politics* 81(1): 274–290.

Goren, Paul. 2004. "Political Sophistication and Policy Reasoning: A Reconsideration." *American Journal of Political Science* 49(3): 882–897.

Goren, Paul, and Christopher Chapp. 2017. "Moral Power: How Public Opinion on Culture War Issues Shapes Partisan Predispositions and Religious Orientations." *American Political Science Review* 111(1): 110–128.

Goren, Paul, and Christopher Chapp. 2024. *Moral Issues: How Public Opinion on Abortion and Gay Rights Shapes American Religion and Politics.* Chicago, IL: University of Chicago Press.

Goren, Paul, Harald Schoen, Jason Reifler, Thomas Scotto, and William Chittick. 2016. "A Unified Theory of Value-Based Reasoning and U.S. Public Opinion." *Political Behavior* 38(4): 977–997.

Hetherington, Marc J., and Jonathan D. Weiler. 2009. *Authoritarianism and Polarization in American Politics.* New York: Cambridge University Press.

Hetherington, Marc, and Jonathan Weiler. 2018. *Prius or Pickup? How the Answers to Four Simple Questions Explain America's Great Divide.* New York: Houghton Mifflin Harcourt.

Hu, Li-tze, and Peter M. Bentler. 1999. "Cutoff Criteria for Fit Indexes in Covariance Structure Analysis: Conventional Criteria Versus New Alternatives." *Structural Equation Modeling: A Multidisciplinary Journal* 6(1): 1–55.

Jelen, Ted G. 2009. "Religion and American Public Opinion: Social Issues." In *The Oxford Handbook of Religion and American Politics*, edited by

Corwin Smidt, Lyman Kellstedt, and James L. Guth, 217–242. New York: Oxford University Press.

Jennings, M. Kent, and Richard A. Niemi. 1981. *Generations and Politics: A Panel Study of Young Adults and Their Parents*. Princeton, NJ: Princeton University Press.

M. Kent Jennings, Laura Stoker, and Jake Bowers. 2009. "Politics across Generations: Family Transmission Reconsidered." *Journal of Politics* 71(3): 782–799.

Johnston, Richard G. 2006. "Party Identification: Unmoved Mover or Sum of Preferences?" *Annual Review of Political Science* 9: 329–351.

Kinder, Donald R., and Nathan P. Kalmoe. 2017. *Neither Liberal nor Conservative: Ideological Innocence in the American Public*. Chicago, IL: University of Chicago Press.

Kohn, Melvin. 1977. *Class and Conformity: A Study in Values*. Chicago, IL: University of Chicago Press.

Kohn, Melvin, Kazimierz M. Slomczynski, and Carrie Schoenbach. 1986. "Social Stratification and the Transmission of Values in the Family: A Cross-National Assessment." *Sociological Forum* 1(1): 73–102.

Krosnick, Jon A., and Richard E. Petty. 1995. "Attitude Strength: An Overview." In *Attitude Strength: Antecedents and Consequences*, edited by Richard E. Petty and Jon A. Krosnick. Hillsdale, NJ: Lawrence Erlbaum, 1–24.

Kustov, Alexander, Dillon Laaker, and Cassidy Reller. 2021. "The Stability of Immigration Attitudes: Evidence and Implications." *Journal of Politics* 83(4): 1478–1494.

Lenz, Gabriel S. 2012. *Follow the Leader: How Voters Respond to Politicians' Policies and Performance*. Chicago, IL: University of Chicago Press.

Lenz, Gabriel S., and Alexander Sahn. 2020. "Achieving Statistical Significance with Control Variables and without Transparency." *Political Analysis* 29(3): 356–369.

Lönnqvist, Jan-Erik, Sointu Leikas, and Markku Verkasalo. 2018. "Value Change in Men and Women Entering Parenthood: New Mothers' Value Priorities Shift Towards Conservation Values." *Personality and Individual Differences* 120(1): 47–51.

Luttig, Matthew D. 2021. "Reconsidering the Relationship between Authoritarianism and Republican Support in 2016 and Beyond." *Journal of Politics* 83(2): 783–787.

MacWilliams, Matthew C. 2020. "Trump Is an Authoritarian. So Are Millions of Americans." *Politico*, September 23. www.politico.com/news/magazine/2020/09/23/trump-america-authoritarianism-420681.

Margolis, Michelle F. 2018. *From Political to the Pews: How Partisanship and the Political Environment Shape Religious Identity.* Chicago, IL: University of Chicago Press.

Miles, Andrew. 2015. "The (Re)genesis of Values: Examining the Importance of Values for Action." *American Sociological Review* 80(4): 680–704.

Milfont, Taciano L., Petar Milojev, and Chris G. Sibley. 2016. "Values Stability and Change in Adulthood: A 3-Year Longitudinal Study of Rank-Order Stability and Mean-Level Differences." *Personality and Social Psychology Bulletin* 42(5): 572–588.

Pérez, Efrén O., and Marc J. Hetherington. 2014. "Authoritarianism in Black and White: Testing the Cross-Racial Validity of the Parenting Scale." *Political Analysis* 22(3): 398–412.

Politico Magazine. 2016. "The 155 Craziest Things Trump Said This Election." *Politico*, November 5. www.politico.com/magazine/story/2016/11/the-155-craziest-things-trump-said-this-cycle-214420/.

Price, Vincent, and John Zaller. 1993. "Who Gets the News? Alternative Measures of News Reception and Their Implications for Research." *Public Opinion Quarterly* 57(2): 133–164.

Putnam, Robert D., and David Campbell. 2010. *American Grace: How Religion Divides and Unites Us*. New York: Simon and Schuster.

Rhemtulla, Mijke, Patricia É. Brosseau-Liard, and Victoria Savalei. 2012. "When Can Categorical Variables Be Treated as Continuous? A Comparison of Robust Continuous and Categorical SEM Estimation Methods under Suboptimal Conditions." *Psychological Methods* 17: 354–373.

Rokeach, Milton. 1973. *The Nature of Human Values*. New York: Free Press.

Ryan, Timothy J. 2014. "Reconsidering Moral Issues in Politics." *Journal of Politics* 76(2): 380–397.

Ryan, Timothy J. 2017. "No Compromise: Political Consequences of Moralized Attitudes." *American Journal of Political Science* 61(2): 409–423.

Sagiv, Lilach, Sonia Roccas, Jan Ciecihch, and Shalom Schwartz. 2017. "Personal Values in Human Life." *Nature Human Behaviour* 1: 630–639.

Schuster, Carolin, Lisa Pinkowski, and Daniel Fischer. 2019. "Intra-individual Value Change in Adulthood." *Zeitschrift für Psychologie* 227(1): 42–52.

Schwartz, Shalom H. 1992. "Universals in the Content and Structure of Values: Theoretical Advances and Empirical Tests in 20 Countries." *Advances in Experimental Social Psychology* 25: 1–65.

Schwartz, Shalom. H. 1994. "Are There Universal Aspects in the Structure and Content of Human Values?" *Journal of Social Issues* 50(1): 19–45.

Sears, David O. 1983. "The Persistence of Early Political Predispositions: The Roles of Attitude Object and Life Stage." In *Review of Personality and Social*

Psychology, Vol. 4, edited by L. Wheeler and P. Shaver, 79–116. Beverly Hills, CA: Sage.

Sears, David O., and Christia Brown. 2023. "Childhood and Adult Political Development." In *The Oxford Handbook of Political Psychology*, 3rd ed., edited by Leonie Huddy, David O. Sears, Jack S. Levy, and Jennifer Jerit, 65–108. New York: Oxford University Press.

Simas, Elizabeth N. 2023. *In Defense of Ideology*. New York: Cambridge University Press.

Smith, Amy Erica, Mason Moseley, Matthew Layton, and Mollie Cohen. 2021. "Learning to Rebel: When Anti-authoritarian Parenting Values Are Endogenous to Politics." Presented at the Annual Meeting of the Southern Political Science Association, January 7, 2021.

Smith, David Norman, and Eric Hanley. 2018. "The Anger Games: Who Voted for Donald Trump in the 2016 Election, and Why?" *Critical Sociology* 44(2): 195–212.

Stenner, Karen. 2005. *The Authoritarian Dynamic*. New York: Cambridge University Press.

Taub, Amanda. 2016. "The Rise of American Authoritarianism." *Vox*, March 1. www.vox.com/2016/3/1/11127424/trump-authoritarianism.

Tesler, Michael. 2015. "Priming Predispositions and Changing Policy Positions: An Account of When Mass Opinion Is Primed or Changed." *American Journal of Political Science* 59(4): 806–824.

Vecchione, Michele, Shalom Schwartz, Guido Alessandri, Anna K. Döring, Valeria Castellani, and Maria Giovanna Caprara. 2016. "Stability and Change of Basic Personal Values in Early Adulthood: An 8-Year Longitudinal Study." *Journal of Research in Personality* 63: 111–122.

Vollebergh, Wilma A. M., Jurjen Iedema, and Quinten A. W. Raaijmakers. 2001. "Intergenerational Transmission and the Formation of Cultural Orientations in Adolescence and Young Adulthood." *Journal of Marriage and Family* 63(4): 1185–1198.

Zaller, John. 1992. *The Nature and Origins of Mass Opinion*. New York: Cambridge University Press.

Zumbo, Bruno D., Anne M. Gadermann, and Cornelia Zeisser. 2007. "Ordinal Versions of Coefficients Alpha and Theta for Likert Rating Scales." *Journal of Modern Applied Statistical Methods* 6(1): 21–29.

For EU product safety concerns, contact us at Calle de José Abascal, 56–1°,
28003 Madrid, Spain or eugpsr@cambridge.org.

www.ingramcontent.com/pod-product-compliance
Ingram Content Group UK Ltd.
Pitfield, Milton Keynes, MK11 3LW, UK
UKHW022126010725
460167UK00020B/437